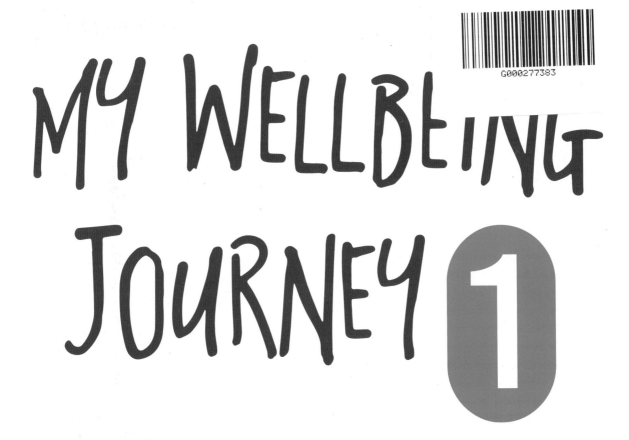

MY WELLBEING JOURNEY 1

Junior Cycle SPHE

**Catherine Deegan
& Edel O'Brien**

G000277383

Gill Education
Hume Avenue
Park West
Dublin 12
www.gilleducation.ie

Gill Education is an imprint of M.H. Gill & Co.

© Catherine Deegan and Edel O'Brien 2019

ISBN: 978-0-7171-84262

Design: Síofra Murphy
Illustrations: Oxford Designers & Illustrators, Derry Dillon

At the time of going to press, all web addresses were active and contained information relevant to the topics in this book. Gill Education does not, however, accept responsibility for the content or views contained on these websites. Content, views and addresses may change beyond the publisher or author's control. Students should always be supervised when reviewing websites.

The authors and publisher are grateful to the following for permission to reproduce copyrighted material:
'The Shepherd, the Sheep and the Wolf' by Ann Irwin O'Leary. Copyright © Ann Irwin O'Leary, a resource created for www.scoilnet.ie.

For permission to reproduce photographs, the authors and publisher gratefully acknowledge the following:

© Alamy; 3C, 51TR, 122, 148CR, 148TR, 157, 164, 166T, 180R: © Cultura; 100, 124C: Courtesy of The Department of Health; 99: © Digital Vision; 44TL, 166B: © E+; 3B, 4C, 44TR, 44BR, 106BR, 112BR, 117R, 123, 124T, 148CL, 148C, 179TL, 179TR, 187TR, 187CL, 187BR, 188: Courtesy of Irish Cancer Society; 119T, 121: © iStock; 4B, 9, 15, 25, 26, 31BR, 31BL, 33, 44BL, 51BC, 51C, 51CL, 51TL, 51TC, 64, 65, 87, 88R, 88L, 94, 104, 105, 106CL, 106BL, 108, 112CL, 112TL, 114, 116, 119C, 143, 161, 173, 179BR, 180L, 187C, 203, 204, 205: ©INPHO/Dan Sheridan; 148TL: © Juice Images; 31TL, 88C: Courtesy of LGBT Ireland; 167L: © Maskot; 148TC: © Moment; 51CR, 112CR: Courtesy of Netflix; 4T: Courtesy of Sherry Matthews Group, Austin, Texas; 117L: © Shutterstock; 3T.

The authors and publisher have made every effort to trace all copyright holders, but if any have been inadvertently overlooked we would be pleased to make the necessary arrangement at the first opportunity.

CONTENTS

INTRODUCTION to My Wellbeing Journey 1

> Welcome to Junior Cycle Social, Personal and Health Education (SPHE)! This is a subject that is unlike nearly any other subject you will take for the Junior Cycle. There is no final exam. Instead, the focus of the subject is on you and your health and wellbeing!

SPHE supports each of the six indicators of Wellbeing:

active   responsible   connected   resilient   respected   aware

For that reason, SPHE and *My Wellbeing Journey* contributes significantly to your school's Wellbeing programme.

SPHE gives you the chance to develop a positive sense of self and the skills and insights for caring for yourself and others. You'll learn to make informed decisions about health and wellbeing and you will develop the resilience needed to cope with some of the challenges of the teenage years.

SPHE and *My Wellbeing Journey* put you at the centre of the learning experience. The active learning methods used throughout this series encourage you to engage fully with the topics discussed. We hope that the activities presented in *My Wellbeing Journey* will make for fun, thought-provoking and valuable SPHE classes.

Catherine Deegan and Edel O'Brien

Using *My Wellbeing Journey 1*

Specification links

My Wellbeing Journey is clearly linked to the SPHE specification. Not only is the book broken into four colour-coded strands but each lesson is linked to a specific Learning Outcome and Wellbeing Indicator. Learning Outcomes are then broken down further into student-friendly learning intentions.

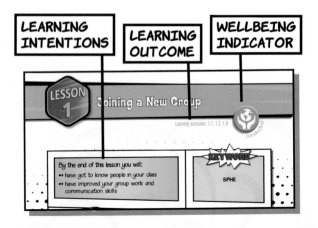

This very clear curriculum mapping will support planning. It will also assist the assessment process as you need to make sure that the Classroom-Based Assessment is based on Learning Outcomes from more than one strand.

Development of Key Skills

Each activity in the book supports the development of at least one of the Junior Cycle Key Skills. Icons indicate which Key Skill is addressed.

Being Literate Communicating Being Creative Managing Information & Thinking Managing Myself Being Numerate Staying Well Working with others

Meanwhile, the words underneath the icon show what element or aspect of the Key Skill is being developed.

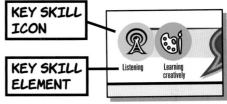

KEY SKILL ICON

KEY SKILL ELEMENT

Listening   Learning creatively

Reflection

Reflecting on learning is an important aspect of the Junior Cycle Framework. The Learning Keepsakes at the end of each lesson provide scaffolding for regular reflection. These reflections are particularly useful when it comes to deciding on a CBA in Second or Third Year and for supporting communication with parents. Additional Topic Reviews are available on GillExplore and provide more opportunities for reflection.

Assessment

Meet the Challenges, linked to specific Learning Outcomes, Key Skills and Wellbeing Indicators and with clear success criteria, help prepare you for the Classroom-Based Assessment. They are particularly intended for people following the SPHE Short Course but provide engaging assessment opportunities for all SPHE students.

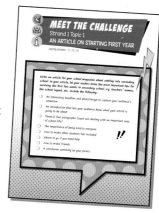

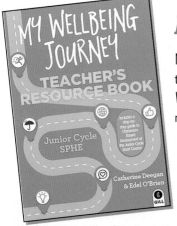

Additional resources

Numerous resources (including videos and PowerPoints) that support teaching and learning in SPHE are included on GillExplore.ie. The *My Wellbeing Journey Teacher's Resource Book* includes useful lesson planning material and schemes of work.

Following the SPHE course using *My Wellbeing Journey*

Your school has a choice in how it implements SPHE. You can:

● stick with the older modular SPHE curriculum (70 hours), first rolled out in 2000

● follow the newer SPHE short course (100 hours), developed under the new Junior Cycle Framework in 2016

● develop your own, purpose-built SPHE short course that meets requirements (e.g. is at least 70 hours long, includes RSE).

All of the choices can seem quite confusing but the *My Wellbeing Journey* series is flexible so that it can be used whatever option you take. The series fully covers both the NCCA-developed modular and short courses. All activities in *My Wellbeing Journey* specifically nurture different Key Skill elements, while all lessons are mapped to relevant Statements of Learning and Wellbeing Indicators, to help ensure you are in line with the Junior Cycle Framework.

How *My Wellbeing Journey 1* helps you fulfil the Learning Outcomes of the SPHE Short Course

The table below highlights where the various Learning Outcomes from the SPHE Short Course are addressed in this book. This list of Learning Outcomes is also important as you will need to make sure that your CBA addresses Learning Outcomes from at least two different strands.

STRAND 1: WHO AM I?

STUDENTS SHOULD BE ABLE TO	RELEVANT LESSONS
1.1 appreciate the importance of building their own self-esteem and that of others	Lessons 1, 2, 3, 5, 33
1.2 welcome individual difference based on an appreciation of their own uniqueness	Lessons 1, 4, 5, 33
1.3 participate in informed discussions about the impact of physical, emotional, psychological and social development in adolescence	Lesson 10
1.4 recognise how sexuality and gender identity is part of what it means to be human and has biological, psychological, cultural, social and spiritual dimensions	Lessons 27, 28
1.5 identify short, medium and long-term personal goals and ways in which they might be achieved	Lessons 6, 7
1.6 apply decision-making skills in a variety of situations	Lessons 3, 4, 6, 7, 8
1.7 source appropriate and reliable information about health and wellbeing	Lesson 9
1.8 explain how stereotyping can contribute to a person's understanding and experience of rights and wellbeing	Lessons 5, 27
1.9 appreciate the importance of respectful and inclusive behaviour in promoting a safe environment free from bias and discrimination	Lessons 1, 2, 5

STRAND 2: MINDING MYSELF AND OTHERS

STUDENTS SHOULD BE ABLE TO	RELEVANT LESSONS
2.1 evaluate how diet, physical activity, sleep/rest and hygiene contribute to self-confidence, self-esteem and wellbeing	Lessons 14, 15, 16, 17
2.2 critique the impact of the media, advertising and other influences on one's decisions about health and wellbeing	See *My Wellbeing Journey 3*
2.3 describe what promotes a sense of belonging in school, at home and in the wider community and their own role in creating an inclusive environment	See *My Wellbeing Journey 2*
2.4 distinguish between appropriate care giving and receiving	See *My Wellbeing Journey 3*
2.5 demonstrate the personal and social skills to address pressure to smoke, to drink alcohol and/or use other substances	Lessons 19, 20
2.6 reflect on the personal, social and legal consequences of their own or others' drug use	Lessons 18, 19, 20
2.7 critique information and supports available for young people in relation to substance use	See *My Wellbeing Journey 3*
2.8 use the skills of active listening and responding appropriately in a variety of contexts	Lessons 11, 12, 13
2.9 use good communication skills to respond to criticism and conflict	Lessons 13, 21, 22
2.10 describe appropriate responses to incidents of bullying	Lessons 21, 22
2.11 appraise the roles of participants and bystanders in incidents of bullying	Lesson 22
2.12 review the school's anti-bullying policy and internet safety guidelines explaining the implications for students' behaviour and personal safety	See *My Wellbeing Journey 2*

STRAND 3: TEAM UP

STUDENTS SHOULD BE ABLE TO	RELEVANT LESSONS
3.1 establish what young people value in different relationships and how this changes over time	See *My Wellbeing Journey 2* and *3*
3.2 evaluate attitudes, skills and values that help to make, maintain and end friendships respectfully	Lesson 23
3.3 recognise their capacity to extend and receive friendship	Lesson 23
3.4 explain the different influences on relationships and levels of intimacy	Lesson 24
3.5 analyse relationship difficulties experienced by young people	See *My Wellbeing Journey 2* and *3*
3.6 describe fertility, conception, pre-natal development and birth, and the particular health considerations for each	Lessons 25, 26
3.7 explain what it means to take care of their sexual health	See *My Wellbeing Journey 3*
3.8 demonstrate assertive communication skills in support of responsible, informed decision-making about relationships and sexual health that are age and developmentally appropriate	See *My Wellbeing Journey 3*
3.9 reflect on the personal and social dimensions of sexual orientation and gender identity	Lessons 27, 28
3.10 critically analyse the use of sexual imagery and gender stereotyping in various forms of media	See *My Wellbeing Journey 3*
3.11 critique the influence of media on their understanding of sexuality and sexual health	See *My Wellbeing Journey 3*

STRAND 4: MY MENTAL HEALTH

STUDENTS SHOULD BE ABLE TO	RELEVANT LESSONS
4.1 explain what it means to have positive mental health	Lessons 29, 31
4.2 appreciate the importance of talking things over, including recognising the links between thoughts, feelings and behaviour	Lessons 30, 32
4.3 practise some relaxation techniques	Lesson 31
4.4 participate in an informed discussion about mental health issues experienced by young people and/or their friends and family	Lesson 31
4.5 appreciate what it means to live with mental ill-health	Lesson 31
4.6 critique mental health services available to young people locally	See *My Wellbeing Journey 2* and *3*
4.7 explain the significance of substance use for one's mental health	Lesson 20
4.8 practise a range of strategies for building resilience	Lesson 32
4.9 use coping skills for managing life's challenges	Lessons 31, 32
4.10 explain the wide range of life events where they might experience loss and bereavement	Lesson 34
4.11 outline the personal, social, emotional and physical responses to loss and bereavement	Lesson 34
4.12 compare how loss and bereavement are portrayed in a variety of contexts and cultures	See *My Wellbeing Journey 2*
4.13 describe how they might care for themselves and be supportive of others in times of loss or bereavement	Lesson 34

How *My Wellbeing Journey 1* helps you fulfil the SPHE Modular Curriculum

The older SPHE modular curriculum is prepared in ten modules, each of which appears in each year of the three-year cycle. Your school can still follow the modular course, if it prefers. However, if you are following the modular curriculum, you'll need to make sure that you are integrating key aspects of the Junior Cycle Framework, such as Statements of Learning, Key Skills and Wellbeing Indicators. As *My Wellbeing Journey* is written to be fully in line with the Junior Cycle Framework, all of this integration has been done for you.

MODULE	RELEVANT LESSONS
Belonging and Integrating	Lessons 1, 2, 3, 5, 21, 22, 34
Self-Management: A sense of purpose	Lessons 4, 6, 7, 14
Communication Skills	Lessons 11, 12, 13
Physical Health	Lessons 15, 16, 17
Friendship	Lesson 23
Relationships and Sexuality	Lessons 10, 25, 26, 27, 33
Emotional Health	Lessons 29, 30
Influences and Decisions	Lesson 24
Substance Use	Lessons 18, 19, 20
Personal Safety	Lessons 8, 9

Additional lessons: 28, 31, 32. These lessons have been written to fulfil the requirements of the new SPHE Short Course. If you are following the modular curriculum you mightn't have time to cover these new lessons and the additional assessment options (Meet the Challenges) provided in the book. Feel free to cover these lessons, if your context allows.

STRAND 1

WHO AM I?

TOPIC 1
How I See Myself and Others

Joining a New Group

Learning outcomes: 1.1, 1.2, 1.9

connected

respected

aware

By the end of this lesson you will:
- have got to know people in your class
- have improved your group work and communication skills

KEYWORD

SPHE

USEFUL WEBSITES

www.kidshealth.org Provides information and advice on starting in a new school.

www.cyh.com Offers information on making friends.

Welcome to your new SPHE class! SPHE stands for Social, Personal and Health Education. In SPHE class you will learn about how to look after yourself, how to get along with others and how to make informed decisions about your health and wellbeing. In today's lesson you will get to know your classmates.

CLASS ACTIVITY

Being social

- You have 15 minutes to walk around the classroom to meet as many students as possible and to ask them a question from the table below.
- Fill in their name and their answer.
- Note that you cannot answer the same question twice.
- When the time is up, return to your seat and read over the answers.
- Highlight any answers you really like.

Name	Question	Answer
dami	If you could travel back in time, what period of history would you go back to?	1986
sean	What country would you really like to visit?	maldives
ko	If you could watch any movie right now, what would it be?	sponge bob
josh	What famous person in the world would you most like to spend a day with?	Ronaldo
ethan	If you don't have a pet, what sort of pet would you like to have? If you do, what sort of pet do you have and what's its name?	hippo
Aine	If you were an animal, which animal would you be?	monkey
Faye	What is your favourite thing to do in the summer?	swimming
eoin	What is your favourite day of the week?	Saturday
Hannah	If you were going to be marooned on a desert island, what three things would you bring?	money, Phone, milky bar
cahal	If you won the lotto, what would you do with the money?	Save it
Isla	Who is your favourite cartoon/superhero character?	Venom

CONTINUED ON THE NEXT PAGE ⟹

③

eoin	Were you named after someone special? If so, who?	no
Maeve	What is your favourite television programme?	Stranger things
lucas	What is your favourite book?	harry potter
éabha	What is the weirdest thing you have ever eaten?	burgers
Robert	How tall are you?	5'4
henry	What is the hardest thing you have ever done?	'I don't know'
grace	Would you rather be the best-looking person or the smartest person?	best looking
ava	If you were at your friend's house and you found an insect in your dinner, what would you do?	take it out
doireann	Do you prefer Italian food or Chinese food?	Italian
lily	If you could change one thing in the world, what would it be?	world peace
michael	Would you most like to be happy, or rich, or famous?	Rich
charlie	Can you sing or play a musical instrument?	no
blathnaid	Who is your hero and why?	a fish
Aisling	What is the funniest thing that has ever happened to you?	a face plant
lexie	Would you rather be too hungry or too cold?	too cold
mara	Would you prefer to sleep in the top bunk or the bottom bunk?	top
carol	If you could change your first name, what would you change it to?	charlie, loti

CLASS DISCUSSION

Discussing/Debating

Making and keeping new friends

Secondary school is new and exciting. It can also be daunting. It is important when making friends to understand how to make friends and what makes a good and lasting friend.

 ## INDIVIDUAL ACTIVITY

Listening and expressing myself

1. Use the letters of the word 'friends' to create a poster that gives advice to students on how to make and keep friends. Use the Word Wizard below to help you come up with your tips.

2. What do you think makes a good friend? Write down three examples of when you might display the qualities of being a good friend.

I am a good friend when I

1. _____

2. _____

3. _____

LEARNING KEEPSAKE

Three things I have learned in this lesson are:

1. _____

2. _____

3. _____

Something that helped me learn in this lesson was:

_____

_____

_____

I could learn even better if:

_____

_____

_____

_____ has shared this Learning Keepsake with me _____

Name of student   *Parent's/Guardian's signature*

LESSON 2

Class Contract

Learning outcomes: 1.1, 1.9

 Connected respected aware responsible

By the end of this lesson you will:
→ have drawn up the ground rules for SPHE class
→ appreciate the importance of creating a classroom environment where everyone feels safe and respected

KEYWORDS

Contract
Confidentiality

For our SPHE class to work well together, we need to have a number of ground rules to ensure that everybody's rights are protected. Sometimes in SPHE class, sensitive subjects can arise. For this reason, it is important that we understand the meaning and importance of confidentiality. Confidentiality means that your privacy is respected and that you respect the privacy of others. As a class, you will agree on a contract with ground rules for participating in SPHE class.

 Remember: **If you reveal something personal in class that your teacher feels puts you or someone else at risk, your teacher must report this to keep you safe. If you feel concerned or sensitive about certain things, it is important that you find a trusted adult to talk to.**

INDIVIDUAL ACTIVITY

Making considered decisions

Confidentiality – respecting the privacy of others and keeping private what they say in class – is one of the most important ground rules for SPHE class. There are other important ground rules, for example:

1. Listening while others are speaking.

2. Respecting other people's opinions.

Add what you think might be three other important ground rules for participating in SPHE class.

3. _____

4. _____

5. _____

GROUP ACTIVITY

Respecting difference

Now share your ground rules in groups of three or four. As a group, decide on the five ground rules you consider to be the most important. When you have decided on the top five rules, fill in the placards. Nominate a **reporter** to give feedback from your group to the teacher.

A REPORTER is the person who gives feedback to the teacher/to the class on behalf of the group.

Listening and expressing myself

CLASS ACTIVITY

Choose a reporter from your group to share your group's ground rules with the rest of the class. The whole class must now agree on a set of ground rules. Ensure each ground rule begins with an 'I' statement, e.g. 'I will listen when others are speaking.' When agreement has been reached on these ground rules, write them into the contract. Everyone must sign their own contract to show that they agree.

CLASS CONTRACT

Signed: _____

LEARNING KEEPSAKE

Three things I have learned in this lesson are:

1. _____

2. _____

3. _____

Something that helped me learn in this lesson was:

_____

_____

_____

I could learn even better if:

_____

_____

_____

_____ has shared this Learning Keepsake with me _____

Name of student   *Parent's/Guardian's signature*

LESSON 3

Coping with Change in Your New School

Learning outcomes: 1.1, 1.6

resilient

aware

responsible

By the end of this lesson you will:

➡ have identified new ways of coping in your new school

KEYWORDS

Change
Solution
Roles

USEFUL WEBSITES

www.kidshealth.org Provides information and advice on starting in a new school.

www.wikihow.com Search for 'how to fit in at a new school' for tips and advice.

www.childline.ie A 24-hour helpline and online service offering information and support for young people and teenagers. **Freephone 1800 666 666.**

A new school brings with it a lot of changes: new teachers, new subjects, a new timetable, new classmates, a new school building. You may be feeling nervous about what lies ahead. This is all very natural. The following exercise is designed to help you cope with the exciting changes you will come across as you settle in to your new school.

INDIVIDUAL ACTIVITY

Knowing myself

Look at the statements and tick how confident you are in each area using the scale.

0	1	2	3	4	5
not confident at all					very confident

STATEMENT	0	1	2	3	4	5
I know how to find my way around school						
I know how to read my timetable						
I know how much time to spend on homework						
I know what equipment I need for each class						
I know how to use my locker						
I understand the school rules						
I am comfortable making new friends						
I know the names of all my teachers						
I know where to go if I need help						

GROUP ACTIVITY

Knowing myself

Below are examples of some problems students may encounter when starting secondary school. In your group, write down solutions to each problem. Nominate a **recorder** to record your solutions to each problem and a reporter to give feedback to the teacher.

A RECORDER is a person who writes down a summary of the main findings of a group discussion.

What could you do if ...

1 YOU FORGOT YOUR LUNCH

2 YOU MISPLACED YOUR TIE AFTER PE

3 YOU NEED TO LEAVE SCHOOL EARLY

4 YOUR HOMEWORK IS TAKING YOU A LONG TIME TO DO

5 YOU SEE SOMEONE BEING BULLIED

6 YOU HAVE YET TO MAKE ANY REAL FRIENDS

7 YOU WANT TO START PLAYING SPORTS

8 YOU LOSE YOUR TIMETABLE

9 YOU FEEL SICK IN SCHOOL

10 YOU LEFT YOUR LOCKER KEY AT HOME

11 YOU LEFT YOUR JOURNAL AT HOME

12 A PERSON IN YOUR YEAR STARTS MAKING INSULTING REMARKS TO OR ABOUT YOU

13 YOU NEED TO SPEAK WITH A SCHOOL COUNSELLOR

14 YOU CANNOT UNDERSTAND SOMETHING THE TEACHER IS EXPLAINING

15 YOU NEED TO GO THE TOILET DURING CLASS

CLASS DISCUSSION

Discussing/Debating

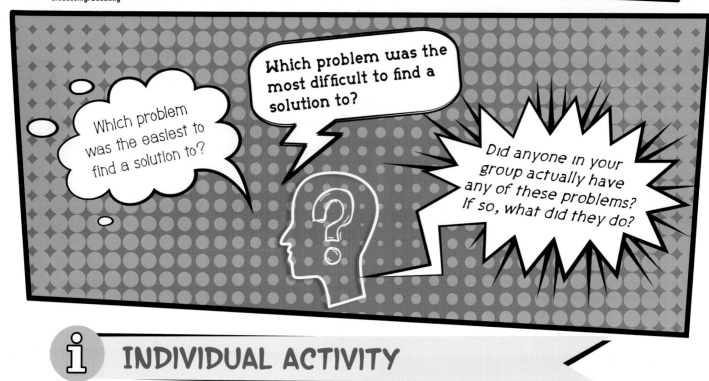

INDIVIDUAL ACTIVITY

Gathering informationa

In the graphic, write the names of each of the people who hold these roles in your school.

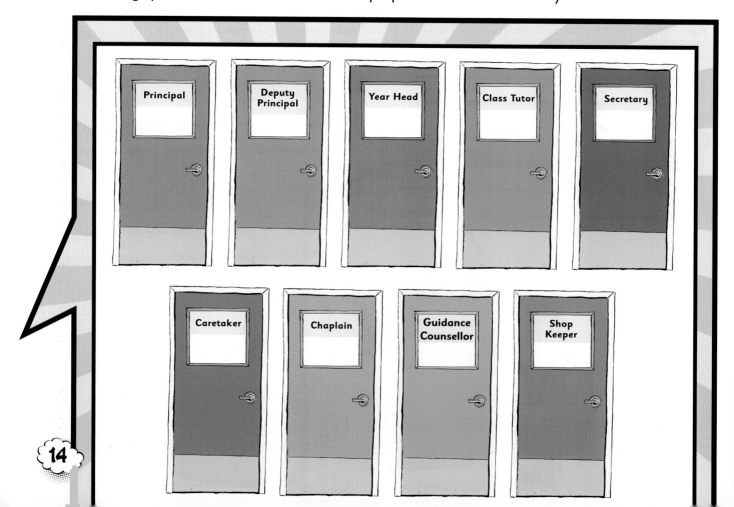

INDIVIDUAL ACTIVITY

Listening and
expressing myself

1. In the sun, write down three things you are looking forward to in secondary school.

1. _____

_____

2. _____

_____

3. _____

_____

2. In the cloud, write down three things that are worrying you about secondary school. Is there anyone you can talk to about what is worrying you?

1. _____

2. _____

3. _____

LEARNING KEEPSAKE

Three things I have learned in this lesson are:

1. _____

2. _____

3. _____

Something that helped me learn in this lesson was:

_____

_____

_____

I could learn even better if:

_____

_____

_____

_____ has shared this Learning Keepsake with me _____

Name of student   *Parent's/Guardian's signature*

Teamwork

Learning outcomes: 1.2, 1.6

 connected

 respected

 aware

By the end of this lesson you will:

→ understand the importance of teamwork

→ know how to be a good team player

KEYWORDS

Teamwork

Decisions

USEFUL WEBSITE

www.wikihow.com Search for 'how to work well in a team environment' for tips and advice.

 # INDIVIDUAL ACTIVITY

Thinking creatively and critically

There has been a huge earthquake and a large community has been buried under rubble. The rescue services arrive and they know that there are ten people still trapped under a collapsed hospital. They have limited resources and time is running out. They know that they can definitely save four people. These are the ten people who are still trapped:

1

A twelve-year-old boy who is a straight A student.

2

A seventy-year-old female with a serious lung condition.

3

A twenty-five-year-old male who looks after his elderly mother.

4

A female doctor whose husband is seriously ill and who has three young children.

5

A male charity worker who has raised lots of money for cancer research.

GO TO NEXT PAGE

A female nurse who is due to retire next month.	A professional male soccer player who has just got a contract with a major club.	A forty-year-old male who loves animals.	A male prison warden who was bringing a criminal to hospital for medical tests.	A young woman who is four months pregnant.

You are a member of the rescue team. You have five minutes to pick four people from the list to be rescued. Give a reason for each of your choices.

WHO I WANT RESCUED	WHY?
NO. _____	
NO. _____	
NO. _____	
NO. _____	

GROUP ACTIVITY

Co-operating

Now that you have decided who you would rescue first, take fifteen minutes to work in your group of four to come to an agreement about which four people you will all rescue first. Assign the following roles to the members of your group.

ROLE	RESPONSIBILITY
CHAIRPERSON	Ensures the group remains focused on the task. Ensures that everyone has an opportunity to speak.
TIMEKEEPER	Keeps the time and reminds the chairperson how much time is left.
REPORTER	Takes notes and reports back to the class.
OBSERVER	Watches what is happening in the group. Notes what is helpful in getting the task finished and what prevents this from happening.

WHO WE WANT RESCUED	WHY?
NO. _____	
NO. _____	
NO. _____	
NO. _____	

CLASS DISCUSSION

Discussing/Debating

Different roles in groups

In the group activity you learned about roles that are helpful when people are working in groups or teams. Here are some other roles that people often take when working as part of a group or team.

1. **Leader:** Takes control of the task and tries to organise others.

2. **Follower:** Does not try to control the task but is happy to participate and follow instructions.

3. **Boat-rocker:** Disagrees with the group and often has strongly held opinions and ideas, which they are slow to change.

4. **Peacemaker:** Offers support and tries to create agreement in the group.

5. **Joker:** Deliberately tries to disrupt the activity and distracts people around them.

INDIVIDUAL ACTIVITY

Reflecting on learning

Record your own and others' helpful and unhelpful behaviours in the grid below.

WHAT I DID THAT HELPED THE GROUP	WHAT I DID THAT HINDERED THE GROUP

WHAT OTHER PEOPLE DID THAT HELPED THE GROUP	WHAT OTHER PEOPLE DID THAT HINDERED THE GROUP

Reflecting on learning

LEARNING KEEPSAKE

Three things I have learned in this lesson are:

1. _____

2. _____

3. _____

Something that helped me learn in this lesson was:

_____

_____

_____

I could learn even better if:

_____

_____

_____

_____ has shared this Learning Keepsake with me _____

Name of student   *Parent's/Guardian's signature*

LESSON 5

Appreciating Difference

Learning outcomes: 1.1, 1.2, 1.8, 1.9

connected

respected

aware

responsible

By the end of this lesson you will:

•• further appreciate the importance of respect and inclusive behaviour

•• appreciate the importance of building your own self-esteem and that of others

•• learn to appreciate your uniqueness and the uniqueness of others

KEYWORDS

Difference
Achievements
Talent
Prejudice
Uniqueness
Discrimination

Although we may be very similar to our friends and classmates, we are all very different in our own unique way. No one is exactly the same as anyone else. We all have our own unique talents, gifts and qualities that define who we are. It is good for us to appreciate our own unique personality and talents, while also recognising the uniqueness and talents of those around us. By acknowledging the qualities and talents in others, we can help them feel good about themselves. We should always compliment others when they are good at something or when they do something well. In this lesson you will appreciate your own uniqueness and the uniqueness of others.

INDIVIDUAL ACTIVITY

Knowing myself

Complete your unique photo frame below by drawing or writing about your unique features in the frames.

Qualities others would use to describe me:

My favourite subject:

Things I am good at:

Things I like:

What I want to be when I grow up:

I would describe myself as:

The quality I most admire in others:

A good deed I have done for someone:

My top two achievements:

1.

2.

23

GROUP ACTIVITY

Learning with others/
Respecting difference

1. As a group, discuss what you have all written about yourselves. Write your answers below.

The talents that are in this group are
The number of people in our group who share the same talent is
The most surprising talent in our group is

2. Sometimes students can experience discrimination or feel excluded due to prejudice. **Prejudice** means judging someone before you know them. **Discrimination** means the unfair treatment of a person or group based on prejudice.

As a group, suggest three ways in which your class could respect everybody's individuality and ensure that everybody is included.

1.
2.
3.

Being social

CLASS ACTIVITY

1. Find another photo of yourself and stick it in the frame below, or draw another picture of yourself. (You can also write your name in artistic writing into the frame if you prefer.) Each person in the class must write a compliment around your picture. The compliment must be about the person's talents and qualities and not about their appearance.

2. Suggest three ways in which you could make others feel good about themselves.

LEARNING KEEPSAKE

Three things I have learned in this lesson are:

1. _____
2. _____
3. _____

Something that helped me learn in this lesson was:

_____
_____
_____

I could learn even better if:

_____
_____
_____

_____ has shared this Learning Keepsake with me _____

Name of student   *Parent's/Guardian's signature*

MEET THE CHALLENGE
Strand 1 Topic 1
AN ARTICLE ON STARTING FIRST YEAR

Learning outcomes: 1.1, 1.2, 1.9

Write an article for your school magazine about settling into secondary school. In your article, let your readers know the most important tips for surviving the first few weeks in secondary school, e.g. teachers' names, the school layout, etc. Include the following:

- An interesting headline and photo/image to capture your audience's attention

- An introduction that lets your audience know what your article is going to be about

- Three or four paragraphs (each one dealing with an important area of school life)

- The importance of being kind to everyone

- How to make other students feel included

- Where to go if you need help

- How to make friends

- A conclusion summing up your points

TOPIC 2
Self-Management

LESSON 6

Organising My Work at Home and at School

Learning outcomes: 1.5, 1.6

responsible

aware

By the end of this lesson you will:

→ be able to organise your homework and school life

Time management
Organise
Timetable

USEFUL WEBSITES

www.kidshealth.org Search 'study tips' for advice on homework and study.

www.how-to-study.com Provides tips and advice on effective study.

GETTING ORGANISED

Now that you are in secondary school, you have a lot more subjects and a lot more to remember. A few minutes spent preparing yourself every night or even at break times can help you to feel more organised and relaxed about your day.

28

INDIVIDUAL ACTIVITY

Knowing myself

Complete this questionnaire to find out just how organised (or not!) you are.

1.   I am on time for school:

   (a)   Always   ☐

   (b)   Sometimes   ☐

   (c)   Never   ☐

2.   My locker is tidy:

   (a)   Always   ☐

   (b)   Sometimes   ☐

   (c)   Never   ☐

3.   I write all my homework, both written and oral, into my homework journal:

   (a)   Always   ☐

   (b)   Sometimes   ☐

   (c)   Never   ☐

4.   I check my timetable every night to make sure I have everything I need for the next day:

   (a)   Always   ☐

   (b)   Sometimes   ☐

   (c)   Never   ☐

5.   I leave homework and projects until the last minute:

   (a)   Never   ☐

   (b)   Sometimes   ☐

   (c)   Always   ☐

6.   I organise my handouts and put them in a folder when I get them:

   (a)   Always   ☐

   (b)   Sometimes   ☐

   (c)   Never   ☐

7.   I can read my own notes and my own handwriting:

   (a)   Always   ☐

   (b)   Sometimes   ☐

   (c)   Never   ☐

8. I give school notices to my parents/guardians on time:

(a) Always ☐

(b) Sometimes ☐

(c) Never ☐

9. I have to ask permission to go to my locker during class to get books or materials I have forgotten:

(a) Never ☐

(b) Sometimes ☐

(c) Always ☐

10. I can find my tie and other clothes I need in the mornings:

(a) Always ☐

(b) Sometimes ☐

(c) Never ☐

Now fill in your scores in the grid below. For each (a), score 10 points; for each (b), score 5; for each (c), score 0.

Question	a/b/c	Score
1.		
2.		
3.		
4.		
5.		
6.		
7.		
8.		
9.		
10.		
	TOTAL	

Interpreting your score

If you scored 0–40
You need to work on your organisation skills. Your school journal and your timetable can help you to do this.

If you scored 45–75
Your organisation skills are quite good. Identify the areas that you can improve and work on them.

If you scored 80–100
You have excellent organisation skills. Keep up the good work!

Managing your time

One of the most useful tools you will use in secondary school is your school journal. It is a very important organisational tool because it allows you to write in your timetable. Your timetable tells you which lessons you will have and gives you information about what equipment you will need for the following day. Your journal also allows you to record and plan your homework in an organised way. It can also help you to record and plan for extra-curricular activities, e.g. matches, choir, etc.

Getting more organised

GROUP ACTIVITY

Learning with others

As a group, discuss the answers to the following questions. Fill in the answers in the spaces under each question.

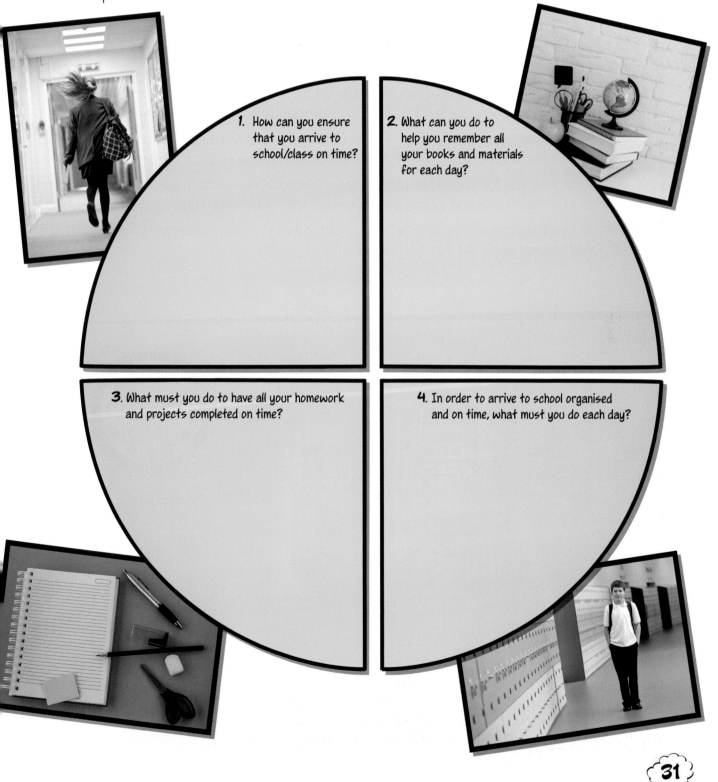

1. How can you ensure that you arrive to school/class on time?

2. What can you do to help you remember all your books and materials for each day?

3. What must you do to have all your homework and projects completed on time?

4. In order to arrive to school organised and on time, what must you do each day?

Tips for getting organised

☞ Keep track in your school journal of important dates. These may include up-coming class tests, term tests, e.g. summer exams, etc.

☞ At the start of each week, take five minutes to record your daily classes for the week. Write in an abbreviated version of the subjects you have each day, e.g. Eng., Sci., Geog., etc. This will help you to be organised about writing in your homework.

☞ Have a notes folder with a separate section for each subject. This can help you keep any handouts you receive in class. Be sure to update this at the end of every day.

☞ If you have a subject on a Monday and you don't have it again until later in the week, write the homework in for that subject on the day you plan to do the homework. Then cross it off when you have completed it.

☞ Get to your locker before classes start in the morning, during break-time and at lunchtime to get the necessary books and materials for all your classes.

☞ Pack your bag for school the night before. Use your journal to make sure you have all the books and materials you need for the following day.

☞ Have a daily 'To do' list, with a list of small things you must achieve in the day, and cross them off as you get them done.

INDIVIDUAL ACTIVITY

Knowing myself

My personal timetable

Using your school journal timetable, pick a typical week at school and fill in what you need to bring in each day.

MONDAY	TUESDAY	WEDNESDAY	THURSDAY	FRIDAY	EVERY DAY

SCHOOL JOURNAL
Name
School
Grade

LEARNING KEEPSAKE

Three things I have learned in this lesson are:

1. _____

2. _____

3. _____

Something that helped me learn in this lesson was:

_____

_____

_____

I could learn even better if:

_____

_____

_____

_____ has shared this Learning Keepsake with me _____

Name of student   *Parent's/Guardian's signature*

LESSON 7

Homework and Study Skills

Learning outcomes: 1.5, 1.6

responsible   aware

By the end of this lesson you will:

↦ have learned about effective study techniques

↦ have created a study plan

KEYWORD

Commitment

Organising Orla

Orla is a First Year student. She has decided to draw up a study timetable for the year. She has a busy social life and enjoys her leisure time with friends and family.

1 Orla's day usually begins around 7.45 a.m. and she leaves the house at 8.30 a.m. to walk to school.

2 School finishes at 3.50 p.m. every day.

3 Orla has camogie training on Monday and Wednesday afternoons from 4 p.m. until 5 p.m.

4 Orla usually walks home from school. Dinner is usually ready at 6 p.m.

5 Orla and her sisters must tidy the kitchen after dinner on weeknights; they have usually finished clearing up by 7 p.m.

6 Orla's favourite TV programmes are on from 7.30 p.m. to 8.30 p.m. on Tuesdays and Thursdays.

7 Orla usually tries to get her homework done before dinner every evening, but if this isn't possible she usually spends an hour before bedtime on it.

8 She sometimes does her homework in front of the TV.

9 Orla is in bed by 10.30 p.m. most nights.

10 Normally, Orla goes to the local swimming pool from 6 p.m. to 7.30 p.m. on Fridays.

11 After her dinner on Friday evening, Orla usually spends a few hours babysitting for the couple next door.

12 Saturday is Orla's favourite day. She stays in bed until about 11 a.m. and then she either goes training or plays a match until about 1.30 p.m.

13 In the afternoon she usually tidies her room or bakes with her mother.

14 Sunday is always spent lazing around or vising her nan.

ORLA'S SCHOOL TIMETABLE

TIME	MONDAY	TUESDAY	WEDNESDAY	THURSDAY	FRIDAY
9.00	English	Home Economics	English	Tech Graphics	Maths
9.40	Irish	Home Economics	History	Tech Graphics	History
10.20	Geography	Tech Graphics	Science	Maths	Tech Graphics
11.00	MORNING BREAK				
11.15	Science	Irish	Maths	Irish	Info Technology
11.55	Spanish	Spanish	Maths	English	English
12.30	Religious Education	Religious Education	Religious Education	Science	Home Economics
13.10	LUNCH BREAK				
13.50	Maths	History	SPHE	Spanish	Science
14.30	PE	English	Geography	Geography	CSPE
15.10	PE	Maths	Irish	Home Economics	Spanish

GROUP ACTIVITY

Gathering information

1. Based on what you know about Orla, answer the following questions as a group:

   1. What commitments does Orla have to take into account before she draws up her study timetable?

   _____

   _____

   2. What changes could Orla make to her study area to make her study time more effective? Give reasons for your answer.

   _____

   _____

3. What is the best time for Orla to begin her homework each day? Write the times into the graphic and give reasons for your answer.

Monday	Tuesday	Wednesday	Thursday	Friday

4. If Orla has a test in Home Economics for her double class on Tuesday morning, when could she fit in some extra study time?

5. What are the things Orla could change in order to give herself more time to study?

2. Choose one day of the week and plan an evening's study/homework for Orla based on her subjects and any other activities she has on that day. Study the timetable carefully in order to see what subjects she may have extra time in which to study because she does not have that subject every day. Be as realistic as possible and try to include short breaks.

TIME FROM:	TO:	SUBJECT

Organising yourself for homework

Here are some ways of improving your study habits. Remember that doing your homework well is a very good way of studying.

- ☛ Keep your study area tidy and organised.
- ☛ Make sure you have all the materials and books you need before you begin.
- ☛ Switch off/put away your mobile phone and turn off all other distractions before you begin.
- ☛ Do your homework in the same place every night.
- ☛ Do your homework at a designated time each night to set up a good routine.
- ☛ Do both written and oral homework. If you have no homework in a subject, read over what you did in class that day.
- ☛ Tick off your homework in your homework journal as you do it.
- ☛ Do not spend more than an hour and a half on your homework in First Year.
- ☛ If you have an important test coming up, make sure that you allow enough time in your study timetable to fit in extra study work.

- ☛ If you are stuck on a question, ask someone at home for help or bring it in as a question for your teacher in your next class. Do not spend the entire evening trying to work it out.

 ## INDIVIDUAL ACTIVITY

Listening and expressing myself

Now look at your own week and answer the following questions:

1. What commitments do you have to take into account before you draw up your homework/study timetable?

_____

_____

2. What changes could you make to where and how you study to make your study time more effective?

_____

_____

3. What is the best time for you to begin your homework each day? Give reasons for your answer.

Monday   Time: _____ Why? _____

Tuesday   Time: _____ Why? _____

Wednesday Time: _____ Why? _____

Thursday   Time: _____ Why? _____

Friday   Time: _____ Why? _____

4. What things could you change to give yourself more time to study?

_____

_____

Study tips

In secondary school, you are faced with the challenge of taking tests. Remembering lots of information from different subjects can be a little daunting. How can you transfer all the information you receive in class and through study to the page in an exam? Here are some useful tips that can make your revision time more effective.

☞ Create a study timetable. When you have a lot of exams coming up at one time, write down how many exams you have and what days you have to sit them. After you have completed your homework, timetable some extra time for exam study. Spread out the time devoted to each subject over the week.

☞ Revisit class material. Read over material you did in class each day, even if it's only for five minutes. This will keep you up to date with what you are learning about.

☞ Don't cram. Leaving all your study until the night before an exam is not a good idea. Research has shown that we retain more information if we break our study periods into 20–30-minute sessions over a few weeks. As the saying goes, 'A little a lot is better than a lot a little'!

When studying a section of a book

☞ Before you start, write down briefly what you already know about the topic.

☞ Read through the material quickly to see what you remember, paying attention to the main headings.

☞ Summarise what you have read by taking notes or drawing diagrams. A mind map is a very helpful visual revision aid. It involves brainstorming around a topic by writing the topic in the middle of the page and then writing the main points around it.

☞ Mnemonics are also helpful memory aids. These can be useful if you want to remember a list of words. This is where you take the first letter of each word and try to make a phrase out of it that you will remember, for example, 'Richard Of York Gave Battle In Vain' could be used to remember the colours of the rainbow.

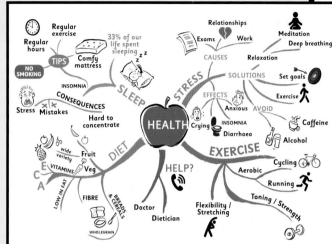

☞ Close your books and notes and test yourself on what you have learned. It might be helpful to get a family member to examine you. This can be good to show up what it is that you still don't know. If you like you could have a list of questions ready for them to ask you.

☞ Read back over your notes again to see what you remember.

 ## INDIVIDUAL ACTIVITY

Managing my learning

Using what you have learned in this lesson, draw up your own study timetable for a week. Remember to include any activities, e.g. hobbies, TV shows, family commitments, etc. that you may be involved in during the week.

TIME	MONDAY	TUESDAY	WEDNESDAY	THURSDAY	FRIDAY	SATURDAY	SUNDAY

41

Learning Keepsake

Three things I have learned in this lesson are:

1. _____
2. _____
3. _____

Something that helped me learn in this lesson was:

_____

_____

_____

I could learn even better if:

_____

_____

_____

_____ has shared this Learning Keepsake with me _____

Name of student ‌ ‌ ‌ ‌ ‌ ‌ ‌ ‌ ‌ ‌ *Parent's/Guardian's signature*

Looking After Myself

Learning outcome: 1.6

By the end of this lesson you will:

➤ have examined ways of keeping safe

➤ be aware of the best response in risky situations

KEYWORD

Risk

USEFUL WEBSITES

www.suzylamplugh.org A website dedicated to help and support people to stay safe in their daily lives.

www.wikihow.com Search 'personal safety' for tips on staying safe in different situations.

www.kidshealth.org Go to the teen section and search 'safety basics' for safety advice.

Although there may be lots of news coverage of tragic accidents and violent incidents, it is important to remember that these things are rare. Nonetheless, as you gain more responsibility and freedom, you may encounter situations that could be potentially risky. Learning how to identify risk and keeping yourself safe is an important life skill.

GROUP ACTIVITY

Being safe   Learning with others

As a group, discuss the potential risks in each of the following situations and write down your answers.

Going out at night with your friends

Being online

Travelling (public transport, cycling and being a pedestrian)

Being home alone

Advice for keeping safe

Read the following tips for keeping safe and discuss the reasons for these with your teacher.

Going out at night with your friends

- ☞ Stay as a group. Don't leave anyone on their own or leave them to get home alone.

- ☞ Make sure you all know how you are going to get home safely before going out.

- ☞ If you know you will be home later than you planned, let someone know.

- ☞ Have a charged mobile phone with you.

- ☞ Stay in well-lit areas.

- ☞ If you feel pressurised to do something you don't want to, stop and think. Don't do anything that will put your safety in danger. Say no.

- ☞ Always have a plan B in place with your parents or guardians in case you need to go home earlier than expected.

- ☞ Don't get involved in fights.

- ☞ Don't ever leave without telling your friends.

- ☞ Never leave anywhere with someone you don't know.

- ☞ Carry spare change in case you lose your mobile phone and need to use a public phone.

- ☞ Carry spare cash in case you need to get a taxi.

- ☞ Trust your instincts. If you feel a situation is unsafe, just get out of there.

Being online

- ☞ Be careful with your profiles. Don't give out personal information such as your full name, school or home address or telephone number. Don't add people you don't know to your friends list; not everyone online is who they say they are.

- ☞ Never meet anyone in person who you only know from being online.

- ☞ Block strangers who might try to contact you.

- ☞ Be careful not to share inappropriate snaps. Use the granny rule: if you wouldn't share it with your granny, then don't put it online.

- ☞ Keep your location private if on social media.

- ☞ If you see something disturbing or upsetting, confide in a trusted adult. It is better to talk about these things than not.

- ☞ If you receive any unwanted emails or messages, tell a trusted adult. Do not respond to these messages.

Travelling: Public transport

☞ When waiting for a bus or train, always wait in well-lit areas.

☞ Sit near the driver of the bus if you are alone. Don't isolate yourself by sitting upstairs or at the back of the bus on your own.

☞ Always have someone waiting for you when you get to your destination.

☞ Note where the alarm is.

☞ If you are getting a taxi, always sit in the back.

☞ Text the registration number of the taxi to a parent or a trusted adult.

☞ Try to book a taxi in advance with a licensed taxi company.

Travelling: Cycling

☞ Always wear the correct safety gear, including a helmet.

☞ Be visible: have the correct lights and a high-visibility vest.

☞ Carry a pump and puncture repair kit with you.

☞ Never cycle too far or into an isolated area on your own.

☞ Where possible, stick to areas with cycle lanes.

Travelling: On foot

☞ Look confident and stay alert. Don't walk while looking at/ scrolling through your phone.

☞ Try not to walk alone late at night or in isolated areas.

☞ Walk facing oncoming traffic.

☞ Wear a high-visibility jacket or reflective belt if walking in the dark.

☞ Never take a lift from a stranger.

☞ Never approach a strange car alone – if someone is looking for directions, let them ask an adult.

☞ If someone pulls up next to you, turn and walk in the opposite direction.

Being home alone

☞ Don't answer the door to strangers. If it's a legitimate enquiry, they can call back when someone else is at home.

☞ Keep all doors locked.

☞ If you have an internal alarm, keep it on.

☞ If you get a phone call from a stranger, don't say you are home alone.

PAIR ACTIVITY

Learning with others

In pairs, read the following scenarios and discuss what you would do. Write your answers in the space provided.

1. You are on the way home from the cinema with a friend. Another group of teenagers approach you and demand your phone. What should you do?

_____

_____

_____

2. You are in the local park. Some of your friends are drinking, and a fight breaks out. Someone has called the Gardaí. What should you do?

_____

_____

_____

3. You are at a party and a friend's dad turns up to collect you both. You feel he has been drinking. What could you do?

_____

_____

_____

Sometimes young people are put in danger by people who are not strangers. What could you do if someone you knew was causing you harm? Discuss this as a group/in pairs.

LEARNING KEEPSAKE

Three things I have learned in this lesson are:

1. _____
2. _____
3. _____

Something that helped me learn in this lesson was:

_____
_____
_____

I could learn even better if:

_____
_____
_____

_____ has shared this Learning Keepsake with me _____

Name of student   *Parent's/Guardian's signature*

LESSON 9

Fire Safety

Learning outcome: 1.7

responsible   aware

By the end of this lesson you will:

→ know the evacuation procedure in your home
→ recognise fire hazards in the home
→ know steps to take to prevent fire in the home

KEYWORDS

Evacuation

Fire drill

USEFUL WEBSITES

www.firesafetyweek.ie Provides useful information on fire prevention, detection and evacuation.

www.wikihow.com Search 'fire safety' for information on fire safety.

Fires in the home are a major cause of deaths every year. But most house fires can be avoided and there is usually a simple method of prevention. It's hard to believe that something as simple as a phone charger, for example, could cause a fire. It is always important to have a fire evacuation procedure at home and at school.

Being safe   Learning with others

GROUP ACTIVITY

As a group, look at the picture below and mark with an 'X' the fire hazards you see.

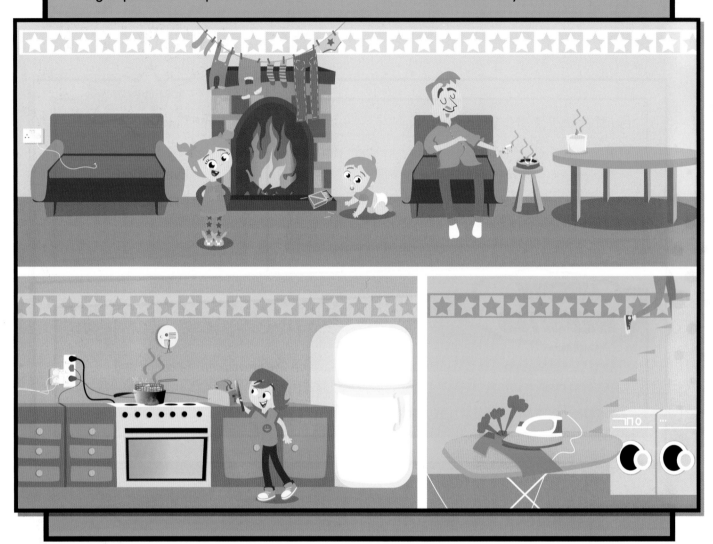

Fire safety

The acronym **STOP** is very helpful in fire prevention.

- **S** is for **smoke alarms**. Make sure you have at least one on every level/floor. Talk to an adult about this.

- **T** is for **test**. Test your smoke alarms weekly or ask an adult to do this in your home.

- **O** is for **obvious dangers**. Look out for fire risks like overloaded sockets, candles and unattended appliances.

- **P** is for **plan**. Plan your escape route. Keep access routes clear and have your keys at the ready.

Fire prevention

You can play a role in promoting fire safety in your home by observing or carrying out these precautions.

Turn off cookers when not in use.

Do not leave a chip pan unattended.

Never overload electrical sockets.

Do not leave a phone charger plugged in without a phone.

Make sure an open fire has a spark or fire guard.

Don't use an open fire to dry clothes.

Never leave candles lit in an empty room. Extinguish all candles before going to bed.

Keep portable heaters away from furniture, curtains or clothes.

Talk to an adult to see if you have your chimney cleaned regularly.

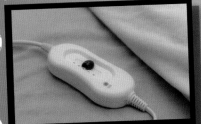

Never leave an electric blanket on for too long.

Close all doors before going to bed.

At Christmas, turn off Christmas tree lights when leaving the house/when going to bed.

Avoid using faulty electrical appliances.

Keep all matches out of reach of children.

Planning your escape route

If a fire occurs in your home, you may have to get out in dark and difficult conditions. This can be especially challenging if members of your family are very young, older or infirm. Escaping from a fire will be a lot easier if you have already planned your escape route and know where to go. This is called a fire drill.

- Involve everyone in the house in the fire plan, including visitors to your home.
- The normal way out is the preferred choice.
- Keep your escape route clear of obstructions.
- Keep keys to doors and windows immediately available.
- Protect your escape route by closing all doors into it, especially at night.
- Practise using the agreed plan.
- Select a safe meeting place outside.
- Make everyone aware of how to call the emergency services or fire service. Emergency services: 999. Fire services: 112.

In the event of a fire

If you discover a fire, or the smoke alarm sounds, react as soon as you discover it/hear the alarm, as you may only have a short space of time within which to safely get out. If possible:

- Close the door of the room where the fire is.
- Do not try to grab any valuables.
- Get out as quickly as possible and **stay out**.
- Once out, telephone the emergency services on 999 or the fire service on 112 from a neighbour's house or mobile phone.
- **Never** go back into a house until the fire service says it is safe to do so.

If you are cut off by fire, try to remain calm

- Close the door and use towels or sheets to block any gaps.
- Try to make your way to the window.
- If the room becomes smoky, get low to the floor. Smoke is hot, so it rises; this means that there is cleaner air to breathe below the smoke level.
- Cover your nose or mouth.
- If your clothes catch fire, stop, drop and roll until you put out the fire.
- If you are trapped in a room, open the window and try to attract the attention of others.

(Source: adapted from www.firesafetyweek.ie)

Being safe

INDIVIDUAL ACTIVITY

Escaping from a fire will be a lot easier if you have already planned your escape route and know where to go. Below is an example of an escape route. Draw a similar map of your own home in the blank box below and design the escape route. Show this to an adult and practise the escape route.

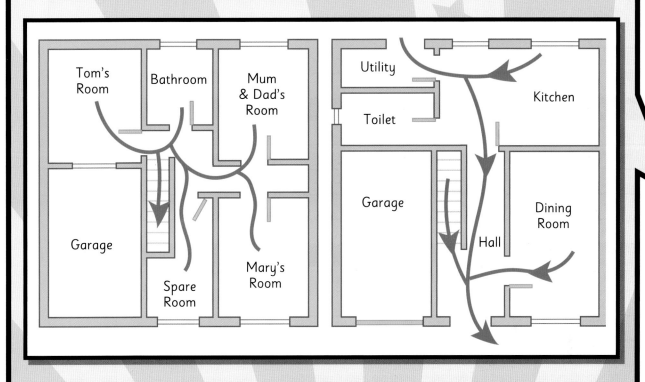

Fire safety checks

From what you learned in this lesson, carry out the following fire safety checks in your own home with an adult and other family members. You should be able to tick 'Yes' to each of the following safety statements; if not, work together to take action to rectify this.

SMOKE ALARMS	YES	NO	TAKE ACTION
1. There is at least one smoke alarm on every floor of our house.			
2. We test our smoke alarm once a week.			
3. We replace the batteries at least once a year.			
4. We never disconnect the batteries.			
5. We all know the sound of the smoke alarm.			
FIRE ESCAPE PLAN			
1. Our family has an escape route.			
2. We have practised our plan and know our escape route.			
3. We all are aware of the safe meeting point outside the house.			
4. We have at least two ways out from each part of our home.			
5. All our family know the emergency numbers 999 and 112.			
FIRE DANGERS			
1. We turn cookers off when not in use.			
2. Our cooker and extractor fan are clean and free from grease.			
3. We do not use our cooker to dry clothes.			
4. We do not leave the room when the chip pan is on.			
5. We turn off and unplug electrical appliances when we are not using them.			
6. We never overload sockets.			
7. Our open fires have both spark and fire guards.			
8. We never use an open fire to dry clothes.			
9. We clean our chimney regularly.			
10. We keep portable heaters away from furniture, curtains and clothes.			
11. We never leave candles lit in an empty room.			
12. No one in our home smokes in bed.			
13. We regularly check electric blankets for any faults.			
NIGHT ROUTINE			
1. We make sure the spark guards are in place on all open fires.			
2. We switch off and unplug electrical appliances before going to bed.			
3. We close all doors at night.			
4. We keep our escape route clear at night.			
5. Keys are in an accessible place that everyone knows.			

(Source: adapted from www.firesafetyweek.ie)

LEARNING KEEPSAKE

Three things I have learned in this lesson are:

1. _____

2. _____

3. _____

Something that helped me learn in this lesson was:

_____

_____

_____

I could learn even better if:

_____

_____

_____

_____ has shared this Learning Keepsake with me _____

Name of student   *Parent's/Guardian's signature*

MEET THE CHALLENGE

Strand 1 Topic 2

DESIGN AND CREATE A 'GOOD STUDY HABITS' BOOKMARK

Learning outcomes: 1.5, 1.6

Design and create a bookmark for First Year students with tips for good study habits. Use both sides of the bookmark and try to make it as attractive as possible. Perhaps you could even use it for an enterprise project in Business Studies and create a business selling your bookmarks. Include tips, as space allows, about the following or anything else you think is helpful:

○ how to set goals for study so that your grades improve

○ how to be prepared for exams

○ how to use your school journal to get organised

○ what kind of a study area to have

○ how much time to spend on homework and study

○ what to do if you cannot figure something out

○ instructions for mind mapping

LESSON 10

Changes at Adolescence

Learning outcome: 1.3

connected · resilient · aware · responsible

By the end of this lesson you will:

➤ understand the changes that occur during adolescence

KEYWORDS

Puberty
Adolescence

USEFUL WEBSITES

www.kidshealth.org Provides information on a wide range of topics related to puberty and growing up.

www.cyh.com Gives an a–z on issues affecting young people.

www.childline.ie A 24-hour helpline and online service offering information and support for young people and teenagers. **Freephone 1800 666 666**.

www.barnardos.ie Provides useful advice on a wide range of issues affecting young people.

Changes at adolescence

Adolescence is a time of great change. You have probably heard the word 'puberty' by now, but what exactly is it?

Puberty is the time in your life when your body begins to change, develop and mature. These changes are necessary to help you become a father or a mother one day. Puberty starts sometime between the ages of 8 and 14 for girls, and between 9 and 15 for boys.

Puberty can be an exciting but confusing – and sometimes difficult – time for teenagers. It is important to know about the changes that happen during puberty so that you can be prepared, and to remember that everyone goes through puberty at different times, according to their own body clock. No two people are the same, and some people will start earlier or later than others. If you are not experiencing any of these changes we will look at now, it does not mean there is something wrong with you.

PAIR ACTIVITY

Learning with others

Below are a list of changes and challenges that teenagers may experience during puberty. Males and females experience similar and different changes. In pairs, write the number of each change written on the wall into the correct space in the Venn diagram. For example, if you think a change only applies to males, write it into the male side. If you think it only applies to females, write it into the female side. If you think the change applies to both males and females, write it into the intersection.

1. Oily skin
2. Growth spurts
3. Mood swings
4. ACNE
5. Conflicting thoughts
6. Wanting to fit in
7. Wet dreams
8. Erections
9. Peer pressure
10. Voice deepens
11. Arguments with parents/guardians
12. Breasts develop
13. Spending more time with peers and friends
14. Shoulders widen
15. Facial hair
16. Want more independence
17. Interest in boys or girls
18. Strong feelings and emotions
19. Getting sexual feelings
20. Greasy hair
21. Feeling lonely and confused
22. Feeling frustrated
23. Underarm hair
24. Concern about appearance
25. Pubic hair
26. Increased sweating
27. Penis growth
28. Increased weight
29. Hips get wider
30. Menstruation begins
31. Eggs are produced
32. Sperm is produced
33. Discharge

MALE CHANGES   **BOTH**   **FEMALE CHANGES**

INDIVIDUAL ACTIVITY

Gathering data

Below are four categories of changes. In the table below, write each change written on the wall in the last task under its correct category.

Physical changes: Relates to the changes that occur in your body.

Emotional changes: Relates to changes in your moods and feelings, which occur because our brains are teaching us how to express our feelings in a grown-up way.

Social changes: Relates to changes in the way you interact with others and in the way you see yourself. You are seeking more independence and examining where you fit in.

Psychological changes: Relates to changes in the way you think. You start to form your own ideals and values in your quest to be more independent and develop your own identity.

PHYSICAL CHANGES	EMOTIONAL CHANGES	SOCIAL CHANGES	PSYCHOLOGICAL CHANGES

Puberty and hormones

Puberty begins when a gland in the brain called the pituitary gland sends a message to the brain to release special chemicals called hormones. These hormones trigger the start of the changes that occur during puberty.

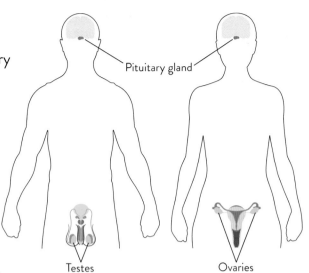

Pituitary gland

Testes   Ovaries

In boys

In boys, hormones travel through the bloodstream and signal the testes to produce testosterone and sperm. Testosterone causes most of the changes in the male body during puberty. It is responsible for muscle development, bone mass and body and facial hair. Sperm cells enable the male to reproduce – to create a baby.

In girls

In girls, hormones travel through the bloodstream and signal the ovaries to produce oestrogen and progesterone. Oestrogen controls puberty and the menstrual cycle. It is also responsible for the development of breasts and body hair. Progesterone prepares the female body for pregnancy, should it occur.

Learning with others

CLASS ACTIVITY

With all these chemicals zinging around in our bodies, it is little wonder that puberty is a challenging time. On the Post-its below are examples of some common questions adolescents may have during this time. Imagine a friend came to you with any one of these difficulties. From what you learned in class today, give them your advice. Only answer the questions you feel comfortable answering or feel you are able to. When you are finished, as a class think of other questions that someone your age might like answered about puberty.

All my friends are going through puberty and I'm not. Is there something wrong with me?

Sometimes I'm in great form and sometimes I feel frustrated and angry. Why is this happening to me?

I feel at times I'm different to others and I just don't fit in. What should I do?

The other boys and girls in my class are always flirting with each other, and some of them already have a boyfriend or girlfriend. I don't feel I'm ready for that yet. What should I do?

I really like a girl in my class but I don't know if she likes me. What should I do?

Every month there is a teenage disco but my father won't let me go. What should I do?

In the last year I don't feel like I'm getting on with my parents like I used to. Why is this? What could I do?

LEARNING KEEPSAKE

Three things I have learned in this lesson are:

1. _____

2. _____

3. _____

Something that helped me learn in this lesson was:

_____

_____

_____

I could learn even better if:

_____

_____

_____

_____ has shared this Learning Keepsake with me _____

Name of student   *Parent's/Guardian's signature*

MINDING MYSELF & MINDING OTHERS

STRAND 2

TOPIC 1
Respectful Communication

LESSON 11

Express Yourself

Learning outcome: 2.8

respected

aware

By the end of this lesson you will:

◆ understand how words, body language and tone come together to help you communicate effectively

KEYWORDS

Tone
Body language

USEFUL WEBSITE

www.wikihow.com Search 'communication' for helpful tips on improving your communication skills.

How do we communicate?

How we communicate impacts on how we get on with people and how we get the things we want. If you do not clearly express what you think or feel, people can misunderstand you. It is important to remember that only 7% of communication is contained in the words we use. The rest comes from our tone of voice and our body language.

How we communicate

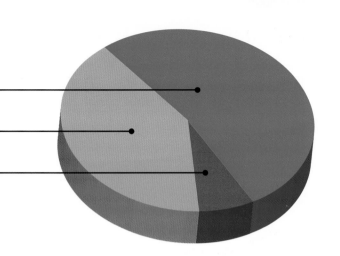

55% = body language

38% = tone (How we say it)

7% = verbal (What we say)

Tone of voice

Many words, sentences and phrases have different meanings depending on the tone in which they are said and the words that are stressed. The tone of our voice and the emphasis we place on certain words can show others how we are feeling. So it is not about what you say, more about how you say it. Sometimes we need to check the tone of voice we are using to ensure we are getting the right message across. It is for that reason that text messages can sometimes be misinterpreted as you cannot 'hear' a tone of voice when you read it. (Emojis can express intention, but they're not always reliable!)

PAIR ACTIVITY

Listening and
expressing myself

1. In pairs, practise saying the following sentence in three different tones:

> I had a great day
> (sarcastic)

> I had a great day
> (surprised)

> I had a great day
> (happy)

2. Now make up two more sentences where stressing different words changes the meaning. Write the examples you came up with below:

Sentence 1: _____

Sentence 2: _____

3. What is the main thing you learned from doing this exercise?

_____

_____

Body language

As you saw in the pie chart, body language makes up the largest part of how we communicate with others and what messages they receive from us. Body language is how we communicate non-verbally, where we use our bodies to convey our message. Body language often reveals our true feelings or emotions, and gives out positive or negative messages to others depending on how we use it. We can be aware we are using body language to convey our meaning, but sometimes we use body language unintentionally.

TYPES OF BODY LANGUAGE

Ways of talking (e.g. pauses, stress on words)

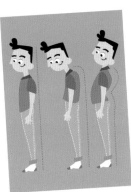

Posture
(e.g. slouching)

Appearance
(e.g. untidiness)

Head movements
(e.g. nodding)

Hand movements
(e.g. waving)

Eye movements
(e.g. winking)

Facial expressions
(e.g. frowning)

Body contact
(e.g. shaking hands)

Closeness (e.g. invading someone else's space)

Sounds
(e.g. laughing)

INDIVIDUAL ACTIVITY

Thinking creatively and critically

1. Pick any three types of body language and write down why you think they are important when you are speaking with someone.

   1. _____

   2. _____

   3. _____

2. Now examine the pictures given here. Write down what message is being given by the body language and say how you know this. Is it appropriate? Why?

   Picture 1

   (a) What is the body language of the boy blowing the bubbles saying?

   _____

   _____

   (b) How do you know?

   _____

   _____

   (c) Is it appropriate? Why?

   _____

   _____

   Picture 2

   (a) What is the body language of the daughter saying?

   _____

   _____

   (b) How do you know?

   _____

   _____

   (c) Is it appropriate? Why?

   _____

   _____

   Picture 3

   (a) What is the body language of the two people saying?

   _____

   _____

(b) How do you know?

_____

_____

(c) Is it appropriate? Why?

_____

_____

Picture 4

(a) What is the body language of the two people saying?

_____

_____

(b) How do you know?

_____

_____

(c) Is it appropriate? Why?

_____

_____

Picture 5

(a) What is the body language of the shop assistants saying?

_____

_____

(b) How do you know?

_____

_____

(c) Is it appropriate? Why?

_____

_____

Picture 6

(a) What is the body language of the business people saying?

_____

_____

(b) How do you know?

_____

_____

(c) Is it appropriate? Why?

_____

_____

Picture 7

(a) What is the body language of the mother saying?

_____

_____

(b) How do you know?

_____

_____

(c) Is it appropriate? Why?

_____

_____

CLASS ACTIVITY

Learning with others

Try to come up with other examples of body language and what they mean, e.g. pointing your finger at someone might mean you are bossing them about.

Remember

To communicate effectively:

- Choose your words carefully: although they are not the whole story, they are important.

- Be aware of your body language: is it sending the right message?

- Take care with your tone: be aware of how you say what you say.

INDIVIDUAL ACTIVITY

Thinking creatively and critically

What tone of voice and body language might you use if you were:

- Annoyed? _____

- Bored? _____

- Excited? _____

- Angry? _____

- Worried? _____

- Happy? _____

Learning Keepsake

Three things I have learned in this lesson are:

1. _____

2. _____

3. _____

Something that helped me learn in this lesson was:

_____

_____

_____

I could learn even better if:

_____

_____

_____

_____ has shared this Learning Keepsake with me _____

Name of student   *Parent's/Guardian's signature*

LESSON 12

Learning to Listen

Learning outcome: 2.8

respected · aware · connected · responsible

By the end of this lesson you will:
- → have practised your listening skills
- → realise the importance of being a good listener

KEYWORDS

Listening
Selective listening

USEFUL WEBSITE

www.reachout.com Provides information on communication styles and good listening skills.

!!

Listening is a two-way process. Sometimes we will be the speaker and sometimes we will be the listener. It is very important to take turns when you are having a conversation. Listening is a skill and can be improved.

INDIVIDUAL ACTIVITY

Knowing myself

Write down the names of the people you have conversations with daily.

_____

_____

_____

_____

Listening

Learning creatively

PAIR ACTIVITY

In pairs, carry out these listening activities.

Listening activity 1: Draw me a picture!

Instructions:

Step 1: Decide who will be A and who will be B.

Step 2: A draws a simple picture into the frame on the left below, using only shapes and lines, similar to the example given on the right.

Step 3: B cannot look while A is drawing their picture. When A has finished drawing their picture, they cover it up and then give oral directions to B on how to draw the picture, which they draw into the frame on the right below. A must not look at B's work while they are drawing. B must not ask any questions.

Step 4: When B has finished, compare the drawings.

Step 5: Switch roles.

Person A drawing

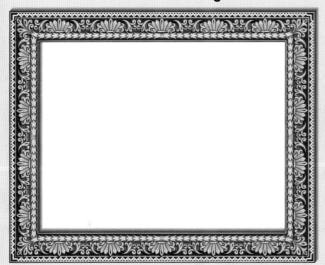

Person B drawing

How did you find this activity – easy or difficult?

Was it difficult trying to describe your line picture to the other person without showing them?

How could you communicate better?

Was it difficult not being able to ask questions?

What do you think would help you draw a better picture?

Listening activity 2: Face to face

Instructions:

Step 1: Sit on chairs facing each other.

Step 2: When the teacher gives the signal, you are to speak to each other for 30 seconds at the same time about what you did last weekend.

What did that feel like?

Was it difficult to hear your partner?

What is the main message you got about good listening from doing this?

Listening activity 3: Back to back

Instructions:

Step 1: Decide who will be A and who will be B.

Step 2: Sit back to back.

Step 3: When the teacher gives the signal, A talks to B for 30 seconds about what they like to do in their free time.

Step 4: Switch roles.

What did that feel like?

Was it difficult to hear your partner?

What is the main message you got about good listening from doing this?

Listening activity 4: Not listening

Instructions:

Step 1: Decide who will be A and who will be B.

Step 2: Sit facing each other.

Step 3: When the teacher gives the signal, A talks to B about their favourite film. B must act as if they're not listening to A at all.

Step 4: Switch roles.

What did that feel like?

What is the main message you got about good listening from doing this?

Good listening skills vs poor listening habits

Good listening skills are when you make the other person feel that you are interested in what they are saying, and that therefore you care about them and what they have to say. Poor listening habits are when the other person feels as if you don't care about what they are saying.

INDIVIDUAL ACTIVITY

Thinking creatively and critically

Below are a number of statements about listening. Tick whether you think each statement is a good listening skill or a poor listening habit.

STATEMENT	GOOD	POOR
Making good eye contact		
Paying close attention to the other person's words, gestures and tone of voice		
Being distracted by other things going on around you		
Interrupting the other person when they are talking		
Not waiting for the other person to finish before you start speaking		
Looking straight at them, using movements and facial expression such as nodding and smiling as they are speaking		
Slouching in your chair when someone else is speaking to you		

	GOOD	POOR
Asking open questions that give the other person a chance to say how they are feeling, e.g. 'How ...?', 'What ...?', 'Why ...?'		
Finishing listening before thinking about what you are going to say next		
Repeating what the other person is saying back to them from time to time		
Yawning and telling the other person that you are bored		
Waiting your turn to speak		
Giving advice regardless of whether it's asked for or not		
Showing you understand what the other person is saying by using statements like, 'Do you mean ...?'		
Encouraging the other person to keep talking		

Five poor listening habits

1 **Spacing out** – this is when someone is talking to you and your mind starts to wander. You are caught up in your own thoughts.

Yeah, that's great ...

I broke my leg!

2 **Pretend listening** – when you pretend you are paying attention by using sympathetic words/sounds such as 'yeah', 'uh huh', 'I know'.

3 **Selective listening** – when you only pay attention to the part of the conversation that you are interested in.

Wait until I tell you about my last trip to the dentist

My tooth hurts so badly

4 **Word listening** – when you do not pick up the clues about how the person is feeling, only the words they say. You do not notice the other person's body language or tone of voice.

5 **Self-centred listening** – when you are waiting for the other person to finish talking so that you can speak. You are more interested in telling your story than hearing what they have to say.

INDIVIDUAL ACTIVITY

Learning creatively

Your teacher will choose two people to role-play the following dialogue between Martin and Ivan. When the role-play is finished, identify any poor listening skills you have observed and write them into the box at the bottom of the next page.

Martin and Ivan

Martin and Ivan are friends. Martin meets Ivan on his own after school.

Martin   (*upbeat, looking down at his phone*) Hey, Ivan! How's things?

Ivan   (*downbeat*) Hey. All right.

Martin   (*briefly looking up from his phone*) What's up with you?

Ivan   (*defeated but not wanting to reveal too much*) Nothing much ... I didn't get picked for the team.

Martin   (*excitedly, looking up from his phone*) Oh, actually, did I tell you – I made captain! I can't wait for the match. I think we've a very strong chance this year ...

Ivan	*(now getting angry)* Yeah, well, that doesn't mean much to me because I won't be on the team.
Martin	*(cutting off Ivan, distractedly)* Yeah? Oh well, that's too bad ...
Ivan	To make matters worse, we were meant to be going over to Old Trafford next month for my birthday, but we can't now because ...
Martin	Talking of trips, I can't wait for the adventure centre trip!
Ivan	I can't go to that ... I can't be asking my parents for money for trips like that these days because ...
Martin	You're joking! All the lads are going. Try to get around them – it'll be great. Anyhow, I'll be putting photos up so you can see all the craic there if you can't go.
Ivan	Right ... Talk to you later.
Martin	Yeah, see you later. And hey, cheer up before then!

Poor listening habits identified

Learning with others   Listening and expressing myself

PAIR ACTIVITY

1. Now in pairs, rewrite the dialogue so that it demonstrates good listening skills.

   Martin and Ivan

   Martin

   Ivan

   Martin

   Ivan

   Martin

   Ivan

   Martin

   Ivan

   Martin

   Ivan

   Martin

   Ivan

   Martin

2. Between you, come up with three rules for being a good listener.

   In order to be a good listener I need to:

   1. _____

   2. _____

   3. _____

LEARNING KEEPSAKE

Three things I have learned in this lesson are:

1. _____

2. _____

3. _____

Something that helped me learn in this lesson was:

_____

_____

_____

I could learn even better if:

_____

_____

_____

_____ has shared this Learning Keepsake with me _____

Name of student   *Parent's/Guardian's signature*

Passive, Aggressive and Assertive Communication

LESSON 13

Learning outcomes: 2.8, 2.9

 respected aware connected resilient responsible

By the end of this lesson you will:

- ✦ have identified and distinguished between passive, aggressive and assertive communication
- ✦ have demonstrated assertive behaviour
- ✦ recognise the importance of assertive behaviour

KEYWORDS

Passive

Aggressive

Assertive

 **USEFUL WEBSITES**

www.cyh.com Search 'assertiveness' for useful advice on being assertive.

www.kidshealth.org Search 'communication styles' for more information on this topic.

Communication styles

When we communicate with others we usually use one of three different communication styles.

1. **Passive communication:** If a person communicates using this style, they tend not to stand up for themselves or express their viewpoints, allowing others to dominate them. It is very important for them that other people like them, so they don't say how they really feel or what they really want. A passive person could be described as timid or a 'people-pleaser'.

2. **Aggressive communication:** A person who uses this form of communication tries to get what they want by bullying or disrespecting others. They always want their own way, usually at the expense of others. They ignore other people's rights or feelings. A person who uses this style could be described as being pushy, mean or a bully.

3. **Assertive communication:** A person who uses this style of communication expresses their feelings truthfully and honestly while also respecting the other person. They stand up for themselves and their rights. They negotiate differences of opinion so an agreement can be reached. An assertive person could be described as confident, calm, honest and self-assured.

> Here is your bike back.

> Thank you for returning it. Have you noticed that there is a puncture on the front wheel?

INDIVIDUAL ACTIVITY

Thinking creatively and critically

1. Your teacher will now read you (or will have you read) a story in which three characters demonstrate these three different styles of communication. Listen carefully.

The Shepherd, the Sheep and the Wolf

Imagine a landscape, dry, dusty and warm, on the side of a mountain. The landscape is dotted with a few trees and bushes and there is a dark forest in the distance. In the forest lives a wolf.

Here on the side of the mountain there are flocks of sheep roaming freely. The sheep are happy doing their own thing – cropping grasses and shyly calling to one another. Occasionally a group of sheep move off together as if by prearranged signal and slowly one by one others fall into line – too timid to stay anywhere alone, some whingeing that the grass is better here, then there, but following anyway.

Suddenly the peace is shattered by the growl of a wolf. Out of nowhere he appears – towering, glowering over the petrified sheep. His vicious stare mesmerises the sheep – they stand paralysed, totally unable to run and save themselves. The wolf snarls aggressively. The sheep tremble and cower close together. Some wag little fluffy tails to beg for mercy. Some just lie down and wait for the slavering jaws to close over their little woolly heads.

The wolf looks at them and thinks, 'What a pushover this lot are'. He kicks a baby lamb out of his way and the feast begins ...

Just then he hears the firm step of the shepherd descending the mountainside. The shepherd is tall and walks confidently – shoulders back, head up towards the wolf, looking him fearlessly in the eye. The wolf snarls in his direction.

The shepherd does not falter. 'Wolf, go home,' he says in a strong voice. The wolf licks his bloody chops. He doesn't like the shepherd being near him. He can smell no fear from the shepherd. The wolf stares the shepherd in the eyes and advances threateningly.

The shepherd stands his ground. 'Go home, wolf,' he says, emphasising every word. 'These are my sheep. You have no business here.' The wolf halts, listening to the shepherd's firm voice. The shepherd looks back at the wolf, willing him with all his strength to go.

The wolf feels the strength of the shepherd and he slinks away. 'I'll come back for my dessert,' the wolf thinks. 'When the shepherd isn't here, these sheep are easy pickings.'

2. Now, in the table provided below, write down the communication style you think each character demonstrates, e.g. passive, aggressive, assertive. Then for each character, list the words you would use to describe them and some of the different types of body language they show.

	SHEEP	SHEPHERD	WOLF
Communication style			
Words that describe them			

CLASS DISCUSSION

Discussing/Debating

The benefits of assertive communication

Assertive communication is the ability to express our thoughts and feelings – both negative and positive – in an open, honest and direct way. Being assertive:

- helps us to feel good about ourselves and others

- increases our self-esteem

- helps us to achieve our goals

- reduces the chances of us hurting other people by being able to disagree respectfully

- reduces anxiety by allowing us to express our feelings in a suitable way

- protects us from being taken advantage of by others

- allows us to give and receive compliments

Using assertive communication appropriately

When being assertive, it is very important to show respect for the other person. If the other person feels they have been treated respectfully, even if they do not get what they want they will feel that they have been listened to and their opinion/request respected.

Sometimes we have to read the situation as an assertive response may not always be the most suitable response. We may have to be sensitive to the other person's feelings; for example, if your father has put a lot of effort into preparing dinner and you don't like it, it is not a good idea to tell him exactly how you feel.

Also, in potentially dangerous situations, a passive response may be the best option to prevent the situation escalating and getting worse for you.

Using assertive communication while having respect for other people's rights does not mean you will always get what you want and you may have to agree to disagree in some situations.

Tips for assertive communication

- **Stay calm:** Breathe normally, look the person in the eye, keep your face relaxed and speak in a normal voice.

- **Avoid guilt trips:** Be honest and tell others how you feel or what you want without making accusations or making them feel guilty.

- **Avoid guilt:** Don't allow others to make you feel guilty for being assertive.

- **Use 'I' statements:** Stick with statements that begin with 'I', such as 'I think ...' or 'I feel ...'. Don't use aggressive language such as 'You always' or 'You never'.

- **Use repetition:** Repeat your point quietly but firmly, paying attention to your body language and tone of voice. Stay calm but confident.

- **Be prepared:** Have a line ready to refuse a request if someone is trying to persuade you to do something you do not want to do.

- **Keep to your point:** Don't be drawn into disagreements that have nothing to do with the issue.

- **Be patient:** Being assertive is a skill that needs practice – you may not get it right all the time.

- **Listen:** Listen to the other person's point of view.

- **Show respect:** Always show respect for the other person.

INDIVIDUAL ACTIVITY

Thinking creatively and critically

Read the five scenarios and write down an example of a passive, an aggressive and an assertive response. Write the response you think each character should give in the speech bubbles.

Scenario 1

Mary's friend asks to borrow her bike. Mary would rather not lend out her bike.

Passive response: _____

_____

Aggressive response: _____

_____

Assertive response: _____

_____

Scenario 2

Glen is waiting for his bus, eating a bag of chips, when a group of boys approach him and ask him for one.

Passive response: _____

_____

Aggressive response: _____

_____

Assertive response: _____

_____

Scenario 3

Ryan is late home for the second time this week, after he had agreed a time with his parents. They are very angry with him.

Passive response: _____

_____

Aggressive response: _____

_____

Assertive response: _____

_____

Scenario 4

Gwen and her friends are trying to decide what film to go to. One of the girls insists on going to a film Gwen really doesn't want to go to.

Passive response: _____

_____

Aggressive response: _____

_____

Assertive response: _____

_____

Scenario 5

Kim is sitting in a fast food restaurant with her friend. The person at the next table knocks a large soft drink all over her by accident.

Passive response: _____

_____

Aggressive response: _____

_____

Assertive response: _____

_____

Learning creatively

PAIR ACTIVITY

You have read a number of scenarios in this lesson; now it's your turn to come up with one. In pairs, think of a scenario that particularly relates to you as a young person. With your partner, role-play an assertive response to the situation.

Learning Keepsake

Three things I have learned in this lesson are:

1. _____

2. _____

3. _____

Something that helped me learn in this lesson was:

_____

_____

_____

I could learn even better if:

_____

_____

_____

_____ has shared this Learning Keepsake with me _____

Name of student   *Parent's/Guardian's signature*

MEET THE CHALLENGE
Strand 2 Topic 1
COMMUNICATION ROLE-PLAYS

Learning outcomes: 2.8, 2.9

In small groups, choose one of the following scenarios. Create a role-play that demonstrates how assertive communication can be used to respectfully express an opinion or deal with criticism and conflict.

○ **Scenario A:** Your group is working together to complete a project for your JPA. One group member does not seem to be doing their part of the project and is always messing around during your time together.

○ **Scenario B:** Your team are losing the final. At half-time a row breaks out in the dressing room as some of the backs start to blame the forwards for the score.

○ **Scenario C:** Your teacher has threatened to cancel an upcoming trip because the lunch area was left in a mess after break.

Try to show the following in your role-play:

○ how listening is an important part of conflict resolution

○ how the conflict can be resolved without damaging relationships in the group/team/class

Think about using props to make your role-play more realistic.

TOPIC 2
Being Healthy

Balance in My Life

Learning outcome: 2.1

responsible   aware

By the end of this lesson you will:

↠ understand the different elements involved in being a healthy person

↠ appreciate the importance of balance in your life for your overall wellbeing

KEYWORDS

Balance
Health
Wellbeing
Lifestyle

In order to lead healthy, happy lives we must balance the different parts of our life equally. The World Health Organisation (WHO) defines health as 'The state of complete physical, mental and social wellbeing, and not merely the absence of disease or infirmity'. So being healthy is about having a balance between your physical, emotional and social health. In order to have a balanced life, it is important to have a healthy diet and manage your time properly between school, work, social/leisure activities, relaxation and sleep.

The Health Triangle

The Health Triangle is a diagram representing how balanced our lives are in terms of our physical, emotional and social health.

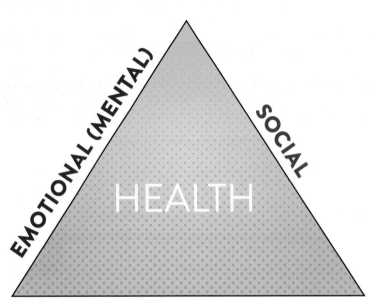

EMOTIONAL (MENTAL)

SOCIAL

HEALTH

PHYSICAL

Physical health refers to our fitness and our ability to perform the physical tasks involved in life as well as sport. It includes having a healthy diet, exercising regularly and rest.

Social health is about how we relate and connect with people in the real world – in face-to-face situations, not in online situations. It is about spending time with our family, friends and other people in our community and in our world, and having respect, empathy and tolerance for other people.

Emotional (mental) health is the ability to acknowledge and manage our feelings. It is about being able to cope with tough times and to bounce back from them. It is also about knowing when to ask for help.

Being healthy   Calculating

INDIVIDUAL ACTIVITY

1. Answer the questions given in the table to examine your physical, social and emotional health. For each statement, answer yes or no as it relates to you.

	PHYSICAL HEALTH STATEMENTS	YES/NO
1	I usually get at least eight hours' sleep every night.	
2	I generally eat a well-balanced diet, including a healthy breakfast each day.	
3	I have good hygiene practices, e.g. brushing my teeth, washing my hands before eating, having regular showers, etc.	
4	I do at least 60 minutes of moderate physical activity each day.	
5	I avoid using alcohol, tobacco and other drugs.	
6	I practise relaxation exercises, such as mindfulness or breathing exercises or other methods.	

	EMOTIONAL (MENTAL) HEALTH STATEMENTS	YES/NO
1	I talk to others about my problems. I don't bottle them up.	
2	I love to learn about new things and I like developing new skills.	
3	I have one adult in my life who helps me when I'm worried.	
4	I am good at receiving compliments.	
5	I feel like I fit in and that generally people like and accept me.	
6	I generally feel good about myself.	

	SOCIAL HEALTH STATEMENTS	YES/NO
1	I spend time talking to friends, putting my phone away to do so.	
2	I'm a good listener, I try to put myself in other people's shoes.	
3	I say no if people ask me to do things I think will be harmful or dangerous to me.	
4	I have a good balance between my school, work and social life.	
5	I respect my family and I spend time with them.	
6	I can disagree with people and allow other people to disagree with me without getting angry.	

2. Draw your own 'Health Triangle' to see if your health is balanced or unbalanced.

Instructions

(a) Your triangle will have three sides, one for emotional health, one for physical health and one for social health. You will draw the sides of your triangle based on how many statements you answered 'yes' to. One 'yes' answer will equal 2 cm, so if you answered 'yes' to four of the statements in the 'Physical health' section, your line for 'Physical health' at the bottom of your triangle will be 8 cm long.

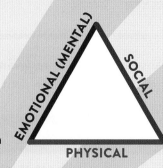

(b) Now draw all three sides of your triangle according to your scale.

(c) Did your lines form a triangle with equal sides? Yes ☐ No ☐ If they didn't form a regular triangle, what could this say about your health?

_____

(d) Write one statement about what you think your triangle says about how balanced (or unbalanced) your life is.

_____

(e) As a result of drawing your triangle, are there any changes you think you could make in your life?

_____

_____

LEARNING KEEPSAKE

Three things I have learned in this lesson are:

1. _____

2. _____

3. _____

Something that helped me learn in this lesson was:

_____

_____

_____

I could learn even better if:

_____

_____

_____

_____ has shared this Learning Keepsake with me _____

Name of student   *Parent's/Guardian's signature*

LESSON 15

Body Care

Learning outcome: 2.1

responsible · aware

By the end of this lesson you will:

↦ know the importance of personal hygiene

↦ have explored the link between good personal hygiene and self-confidence

KEYWORDS

Hygiene

Perspiration

Hygiene

Being healthy

INDIVIDUAL ACTIVITY

Look at the different parts of the body labelled below. For each body part, describe the personal hygiene steps that need to be taken and how often.

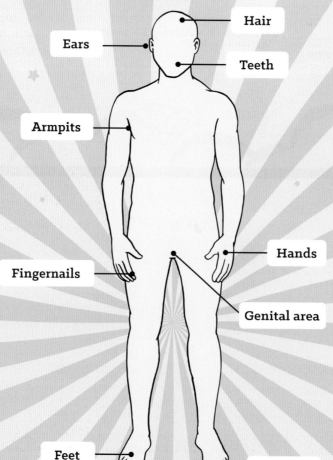

Hair

Ears

Teeth

Armpits

Fingernails

Hands

Genital area

Feet

Toenails

92

Being healthy

As a group, answer the following questions.

1. Why is it particularly important for teenagers to appreciate the need for personal hygiene?

_____

_____

_____

2. How do teenagers learn about personal hygiene?

_____

_____

3. What might prevent a teenager from having good personal hygiene? How could this be resolved?

_____

_____

_____

4. What could/should you do if someone you knew had poor personal hygiene? What would you need to consider before deciding what to do?

_____

_____

5. Under the headings below, list the reasons why it is important to have good personal hygiene.

PHYSICAL – your body	EMOTIONAL – how you feel	SOCIAL – your relationships with others

Why personal hygiene is important

Good personal hygiene is important for our physical, emotional and social wellbeing. The following areas require attention in order to maintain good personal hygiene.

Body

It is important for teenagers to shower every day to prevent body odour. Sweat, which regulates the body's temperature, is formed when the body gets too warm. Body odour (BO) is caused when sweat comes into contact with germs on the skin. Regular showering, combined with using a deodorant or antiperspirant, can help to prevent BO. Roll-on deodorants and antiperspirants are kinder to the environment than sprays. Antiperspirants are more effective than deodorants for dealing with BO. Whichever is chosen, it must be used in addition to showering.

Clothes

Underwear and socks should be changed every day to reduce the build-up of germs that can lead to BO. It is also important to wear clean clothes that have been dried properly.

Skin

It is natural for teenagers to get spots. During puberty the oil glands in skin become more active, so skin care is particularly important at this age. Medicated pads or creams, which can be bought from a pharmacy, can help with spots. It is important not to touch skin as it spreads bacteria, or pick at spots as it can lead to bleeding or scarring. Acne is a skin condition that occurs during puberty. It takes different forms and can be minor or more severe. It is not caused by poor hygiene, but it is important to take good care of your skin if you have acne. In some cases, it may be necessary to seek the advice of your doctor in dealing with acne.

Hair

Hair should be washed at least once a week. If the hair is greasy it might have to be washed more often. Always comb hair thoroughly and check your hair regularly for head lice. An itchy scalp can be a sign of dandruff or head lice. A pharmacist will give advice on suitable treatments.

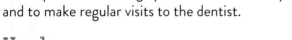

Teeth

Make sure you brush your teeth in the morning and at night. It is important to change your toothbrush every three months and to make regular visits to the dentist.

Hands

It is important to wash your hands regularly to prevent germs spreading. You should always wash your hands after using the toilet and before and after handling food.

INDIVIDUAL ACTIVITY

Thinking creatively and critically

Read about Becky and Brandon and answer the questions that follow.

The Terrible Twins

Becky

Becky leaves it until the last minute to get up every morning. Sometimes she doesn't have time to wash or brush her teeth before going to school. On cold mornings she leaves her pyjamas on under her uniform. Becky showers and washes her hair once a week. When her hair gets greasy she uses dry shampoo. She wears make-up, but sometimes she is too tired to take it off at night. She doesn't always put her clothes out in time to be washed. She sometimes has to pick up clothes from her bedroom floor to wear – including underwear and socks.

Brandon

Brandon spends a lot of time in front of the mirror squeezing spots and he doesn't wash his hands. His mother tries to encourage him to wash every day, but sometimes he just couldn't be bothered. This means that he has smelly feet and armpits. Brandon plays a lot of sport, but he doesn't wash his sports gear until the end of every school term. He doesn't always shower after training or matches, and he has often gone to bed with muck still on him. He lost his toothbrush two weeks ago when he went to stay with a friend and now he cleans his teeth with his finger.

1. Do you think Becky and Brandon's hygiene practices are normal? Give reasons for your answer.

   _____

   _____

   _____

2. How do you think people might react to Becky and Brandon?

   _____

   _____

   _____

3. Do you think their hygiene practices could have an effect on how they feel about themselves?

   _____

4. What might cause someone to have poor hygiene standards?

   _____

   _____

5. Is it difficult to give someone advice about their personal hygiene? Give reasons for your answer.

   _____

   _____

95

Hygiene crossword

Across

4 An itchy scalp may mean you have this condition.

5 A skin condition that can occur during puberty.

6 Regulates the body temperature.

7 You should change your toothbrush every _____ months.

Down

1 This is more effective than a deodorant at preventing odour.

2 These pads can help prevent spots.

3 Spots occur when these become blocked with dirt and grease.

4 Consult this person if acne is severe.

LEARNING KEEPSAKE

Three things I have learned in this lesson are:

1. _____

2. _____

3. _____

Something that helped me learn in this lesson was:

_____

_____

_____

I could learn even better if:

_____

_____

_____

_____ has shared this Learning Keepsake with me _____

Name of student   *Parent's/Guardian's signature*

LESSON 16

Healthy Eating

Learning outcome: 2.1

responsible

aware

By the end of this lesson you will:

→ understand what a balanced diet is

→ appreciate the relationship between a balanced diet and good health

→ have evaluated how diet can contribute to self-confidence, self-esteem and wellbeing

KEYWORDS

Food pyramid

Portions

USEFUL WEBSITES

www.safefood.eu Provides information and tips on nutrition and food safety.

www.hse.ie Search 'healthy eating guidelines' for up-to-date information on healthy eating.

www.bordbia.ie Gives detailed information on healthy eating and the food pyramid.

Our diet plays an essential role in our overall health and levels of wellbeing. A healthy, balanced diet is important during adolescence as this is a time when the body is developing and growing quickly. A balanced diet contains the recommended amounts of carbohydrates (including fibre), fats, proteins, vitamins and minerals, and water.

Eating a healthy and balanced diet helps us to feel good, maintain a healthy weight and perform better in school. In the long term, a healthy, balanced diet can reduce our risk of chronic diseases such as heart disease, diabetes, osteoporosis and some cancers.

Being healthy **Knowing myself**

INDIVIDUAL ACTIVITY

Write down everything you ate and drank yesterday.

BREAKFAST	LUNCH	DINNER

MID-MORNING SNACK	AFTERNOON SNACK	EVENING SNACK

DRINKS

The Food Pyramid

The food pyramid is a visual representation of how different foods and drinks can contribute towards a healthy, balanced diet. It organises foods into five main shelves. This division allows individuals the flexibility to choose foods and drinks from each shelf depending on their food choices.

Food shelf facts

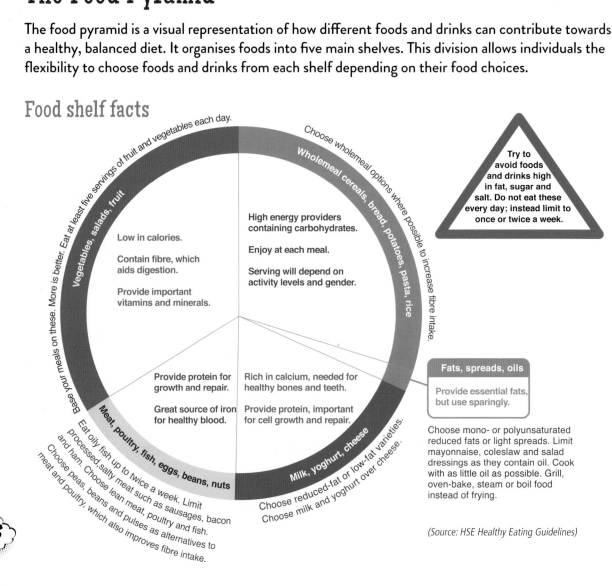

(Source: HSE Healthy Eating Guidelines)

The **Food Pyramid**

For adults, teenagers and children aged five and over

www.healthyireland.ie

Not needed for good health.

Foods and drinks high in fat, sugar and salt

! Most people consume snacks high in fat, sugar and salt and sugar sweetened drinks up to 6 times a day (Healthy Ireland Survey 2016). There are no recommended servings for Top Shelf foods and drinks because they are not needed for good health.

1 serving size is:

(NOT every day)

Small or fun-size servings of chocolate, biscuits, cakes, sweets, crisps and other savoury snacks, ice cream and sugary drinks – **not every day, maximum once or twice a week.**

Fats, spreads and oils

Use as little as possible. Choose mono or polyunsaturated reduced-fat or light spreads. Choose rapeseed, olive, canola, sunflower or corn oils. Limit mayonnaise, coleslaw and salad dressings as they also contain oil. Always cook with as little fat or oil as possible – grilling, oven-baking, steaming, boiling or stir-frying.

(In very small amounts)

1 portion pack reduced-fat or light spread for 2 slices of bread
1 teaspoon oil per person when cooking

Meat, poultry, fish, eggs, beans and nuts

Choose lean meat, poultry (without skin) and fish. Eat oily fish up to twice a week. Choose eggs, beans and nuts. Limit processed salty meats such as sausages, bacon and ham.

2 Servings a day

50–75g cooked lean beef, lamb, pork, mince or poultry (half size of palm of hand)
100g cooked fish, soya or tofu
¾ cup beans or lentils
2 eggs
40g unsalted nuts or seeds

Milk, yogurt and cheese

Choose reduced-fat or low-fat varieties. Choose low-fat milk and yogurt more often than cheese. Enjoy cheese in small amounts. Women who are pregnant or breastfeeding need 3 servings a day.

3 Servings a day — **5** for children age 9–12 and teenagers age 13–18

1 glass (200ml) milk
1 carton (125g) yogurt
1 bottle (200ml) yogurt drink
2 thumbs (25g) hard or semi-hard cheese such as cheddar or edam
2 thumbs (25g) soft cheese such as brie or camembert

Wholemeal cereals and breads, potatoes, pasta and rice

Wholemeal and wholegrain cereals are best. Enjoy at each meal. The number of servings depends on age, size, if you are a man or a woman and on activity levels. Watch your serving size and use the Daily Servings Guide below.*

3–5* Servings a day — **Up to 7*** for teenage boys and men age 19–50

2 thin slices wholemeal bread,
1½ slices wholemeal soda bread or 1 pitta pocket
½ cup dry porridge oats or
½ cup unsweetened muesli
1 cup flaked type breakfast cereal
1 cup cooked rice, pasta, noodles or cous cous
2 medium or 4 small potatoes, 1 cup yam or plantain

Vegetables, salad and fruit

Base your meals on these and enjoy a variety of colours. More is better. Limit fruit juice to unsweetened, once a day.

5–7 Servings a day

1 medium sized fruit – apple, orange, pear or banana
2 small fruits – plums, kiwis or mandarin oranges
Small fruits – 6 strawberries, 10 grapes or 16 raspberries
1 bowl salad – lettuce, tomato, cucumber
½ cup cooked vegetables – fresh or frozen
1 bowl homemade vegetable soup
150ml unsweetened fruit juice

Needed for good health. Enjoy a variety every day.

Serving size guide

Cereals, cooked rice and pasta, and vegetables, salad and fruit
Use a 200ml disposable plastic cup to guide serving size.

Cheese
Use two thumbs, width and depth to guide serving size.

Meat, poultry, fish
The palm of the hand, width and depth without fingers and thumbs, shows how much you need in a day.

Reduced-fat spread
Portion packs found in cafes can guide the amount you use. One pack should be enough for two slices of bread.

Oils
Use one teaspoon of oil per person when cooking or in salads.

Drink at least 8 cups of fluid a day – water is best

Get Active!
To maintain a healthy weight adults need at least 30 minutes a day of moderate activity on 5 days a week (or 150 minutes a week); children need to be active at a moderate to vigorous level for at least 60 minutes every day.

---

*Daily Servings Guide – wholemeal cereals and breads, potatoes, pasta and rice

Active	Child (5–12)	Teenager (13–18)	Adult (19–50)	Adult (51+)	Inactive	Teenager (13–18)	Adult (19–50)	Adult (51+)
	3–4	4	4–5	3–4		3	3–4	3
	3–5	5–7	5–7	4–5		4–5	4–6	4

There is no guideline for inactive children as it is essential that all children are active.

Average daily calorie needs for all foods and drinks for adults

Active 2000kcal **Inactive** 1800kcal
Active 2500kcal **Inactive** 2000kcal

Source: Department of Health. December 2016.

Tips for healthy eating

👉 Don't skip breakfast.

👉 Eat regular meals, e.g. breakfast, midday and evening meals. Try not to leave more than 4–5 hours between main meals.

👉 Limit all fats, including saturated and unsaturated fats. Limit high-fat meals (e.g. chips, battered fish, pastry-based dishes, creamy sauces, desserts).

👉 Taste food before adding salt. Try other flavourings such as pepper or herbs.

👉 Cut down on sugar. It is recommended that we limit our consumption of sugar to six teaspoons per day, but this includes sugar in the foods we eat, not just what we add to our foods, so be careful. (For example, sauces such as tomato ketchup, brown sauce and mayonnaise contain a lot of sugar.)

👉 Drink the equivalent of eight to ten glasses of water each day.

Supplements

If you eat a varied and balanced diet, there will be no need to take food supplements; you will get everything you need from your food. The exception to this is folic acid – all women seeking to become pregnant should take a folic acid supplement, before pregnancy and for the first twelve weeks of pregnancy.

INDIVIDUAL ACTIVITY

Being healthy   Knowing myself

1. Look again at what you ate yesterday. Write or draw what you ate on the correct shelf of your own food pyramid. (For example, if you ate a 125 g yoghurt, write or draw a carton of yoghurt on the 'Milk, yoghurt, cheese' shelf. This would represent one serving of this food group.) Remember to include any snacks you had during the day. Some foods contain foods from a few shelves, e.g. pizza. In this instance, place the different food types contained in that item on the different shelves.

2. When you have finished filling in your food pyramid, add up the total number of servings you had for each shelf, and place them in the box beside the shelf. Compare these to the servings recommended by the food pyramid on the previous page.

3. Fill in how many glasses of water you had in the glass.

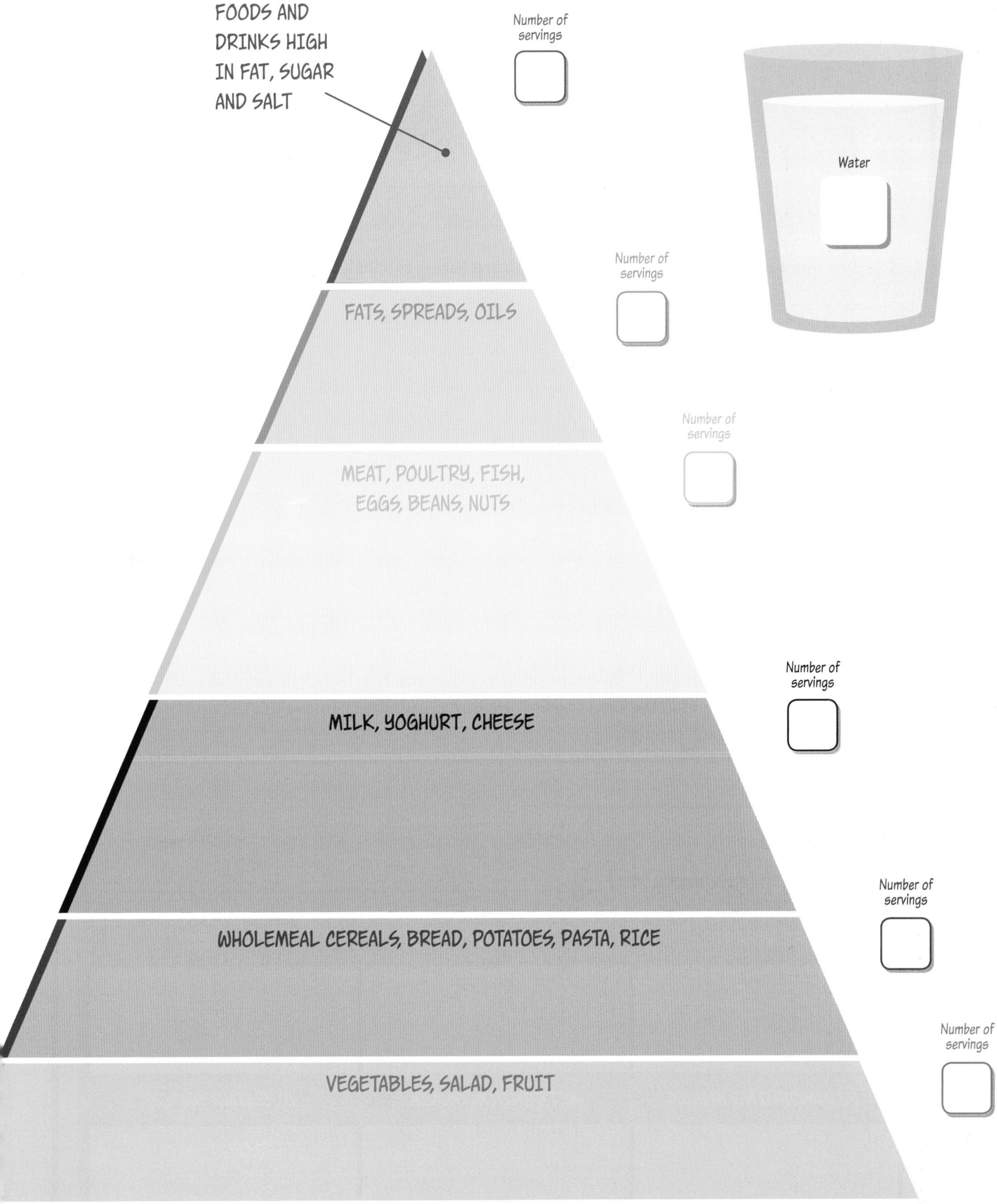

FOODS AND
DRINKS HIGH
IN FAT, SUGAR
AND SALT

Number of
servings

Water

Number of
servings

FATS, SPREADS, OILS

Number of
servings

MEAT, POULTRY, FISH,
EGGS, BEANS, NUTS

Number of
servings

MILK, YOGHURT, CHEESE

Number of
servings

WHOLEMEAL CEREALS, BREAD, POTATOES, PASTA, RICE

Number of
servings

VEGETABLES, SALAD, FRUIT

4. **Based on your food pyramid, answer these questions:**

(a) What does your pyramid tell you about your diet?

_____

_____

(b) Are there any food groups from which you are eating too much?

_____

_____

(c) Are there any food groups from which you are eating too little?

_____

_____

(d) Why is it important not to eat too many foods from the top shelf?

_____

_____

(e) What do you think prevents people from eating healthily?

_____

_____

5. Use the food pyramid guidelines to create your own healthy daily meal plan. Write down what you choose to eat for each mealtime below. Remember to have the recommended number of servings for each food group. Write down the number of servings of each food group you select in the mini food pyramid to ensure you achieve the recommended daily amount of each food group.

Name: _____

Age: _____

Level of activity: (daily/weekly, etc.) _____

BREAKFAST	LUNCH	DINNER

MID-MORNING SNACK	AFTERNOON SNACK	EVENING SNACK

DRINKS

Food and drinks high in fat, sugar and salt
not every day – maximum once or twice a week

Food Pyramid Shelves		Number of servings per day
Fats, spreads and oils		In very small amounts
Meat, poultry, fish, eggs, beans and nuts	2	
Milk, yoghurt and cheese	3	
Wholemeal cereals and breads, potatoes, pasta and rice	3–5	Up to 7 for teenage boys and men age 19–50
Vegetables, salad and fruit	5–7	

LEARNING KEEPSAKE

Three things I have learned in this lesson are:

1. _____

2. _____

3. _____

Something that helped me learn in this lesson was:

_____

_____

_____

I could learn even better if:

_____

_____

_____

_____ has shared this Learning Keepsake with me _____

Name of student   *Parent's/Guardian's signature*

103

LESSON 17

Physical Activity

Learning outcome: 2.1

active   responsible   aware

By the end of this lesson you will:

→ identify the contribution of physical activity to your overall wellbeing

→ recognise the effects of physical activity on your body and heart rate

→ set goals to improve your level of physical activity

KEYWORDS

Recommended

Moderate activity

Vigorous activity

USEFUL WEBSITE

www.getirelandactive.ie A website dedicated to promoting the importance of having an active lifestyle, providing useful tips on how to get and stay active.

As well as a healthy diet, regular exercise along with adequate rest and sleep are very important to overall health and wellbeing. Regular exercise contributes not only to a healthy, well-functioning body, both inside and out, but also to a healthy mind, while adequate downtime and sleep promote recovery – all important factors in promoting physical and mental wellbeing.

Being active

Physical activity has many benefits for our overall health and wellbeing. As a group, come up with as many benefits of physical activity as you can think of. Write them in the box.

Benefits of physical activity

The effects of exercise on your body

Checking your pulse rate at rest, during exercise and immediately after exercise can give you useful information about your overall fitness levels and can show the effect physical exercise can have on your body.

How to check your pulse

You can find your pulse in a few places on your body. The easiest place to check your pulse is on your wrist or your neck.

To measure pulse on your wrist:

- Hold your hand in front of you.

- Gently place two fingers of your other hand (any two except your thumb, because your thumb has its own pulse) at the top of your wrist.

- Move your fingers until you feel a steady beat.

- Count the number of beats for 15 seconds, then multiply that number by 4 to get your pulse rate per minute. For example, if you counted 20 beats during the 15 seconds your pulse is 80 bpm (beats per minute).

To measure pulse on your neck:

- Gently place two fingers (not your thumb) just below your jaw and to either side of your windpipe.

- Move your fingers until you feel a steady beat.

- Count the beats for 15 seconds, then multiply that number by 4 to get your pulse rate per minute.

INDIVIDUAL ACTIVITY

Gathering data

1. Measure your heart rate before exercise now using either the wrist or the neck method.

   My heart rate before exercise is _____ bpm.

2. On your teacher's command, you are now going to jog on the spot for two minutes. As soon as you stop you will take your pulse again.

   My heart rate before exercise is _____ bpm.

   (a) How has your heart rate changed? _____

   _____

   (b) What other differences did you notice in your body after the activity?

   _____

Your resting heart rate is the number of beats per minute of your heart at complete rest. It is best to take your resting heart rate first thing in the morning. As you get fitter, your resting heart rate should decrease. This is because your heart gets more efficient at pumping blood around the body. At rest, more blood can be pumped around with each beat, therefore fewer beats per minute are needed.

During exercise, our hearts beat faster to pump more blood containing oxygen to the working muscles. Like any muscle, the heart needs to be exercised to become stronger. Any exercise that raises your heart rate and makes you feel warm helps to strengthen your heart. It is recommended that you do 60 minutes of physical activity every day at a moderate to vigorous intensity level to stay healthy.

Four out of five children in the Republic of Ireland are not getting the daily recommended amount of physical activity. Only 12% of post-primary students are physically active for 60 minutes every day. Adolescents are spending more time in front of the computer, watching TV or on their phones. This has implications for our health and wellbeing.

Levels of exercise

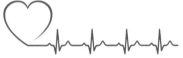

MODERATE INTENSITY	VIGOROUS INTENSITY
When exercising at a moderate intensity level:	When exercising at a vigorous intensity level:
● your breathing is quicker than normal, but you are not out of breath	● your breathing is deep and rapid
● you develop a light sweat after about ten minutes	● you start sweating a few minutes into the activity
● you could carry out a conversation but you wouldn't be able to sing	● you can only say a few words without taking a breath
● your heart beats faster than normal	● it's difficult to hold a conversation
	● your heart beats much faster than normal

PAIR ACTIVITY

Learning with others

In pairs, come up with and then write down as many moderate and vigorous intensity activities as you can think of.

MODERATE INTENSITY ACTIVITIES	VIGOROUS INTENSITY ACTIVITIES

INDIVIDUAL ACTIVITY

Setting and achieving goals

Being active

1. In order to achieve the recommended daily amount of exercise, it is important to set goals. You are now going to draw up an exercise plan for the next week. Before you draw up your plan, note the following:

   ● You do not have to do the recommended sixty minutes per day all at once; you can break it up into shorter bouts over the course of the day, for example:

     ▶ cycling to school = 15 mins
     ▶ playing basketball at break = 15 mins
     ▶ having a kick-about = 10 mins
     ▶ vacuuming your bedroom = 10 mins
     ▶ walking your dog = 10 mins

   ● Choose activities that you enjoy doing.

   ● If you are not normally physically active, start slowly and build up to the sixty minutes.

   ● Taking part in regular physical activity with a friend can help keep you motivated.

   ● Keep track of your progress and tick off the activities as you complete them.

2. Now in the physical activity planner below, write in the activities you plan to do for the next week, and how much time you aim to spend on each activity. Record your progress and say how you felt after each activity

MY PHYSICAL ACTIVITY PLANNER

	Activities I plan to do	Activities I completed	Planned time for each activity	Actual time on each activity	How I felt after activity
Monday					
Tuesday					
Wednesday					
Thursday					
Friday					
Saturday					
Sunday					

LEARNING KEEPSAKE

Three things I have learned in this lesson are:

1. _____

2. _____

3. _____

Something that helped me learn in this lesson was:

_____

_____

_____

I could learn even better if:

_____

_____

_____

_____ has shared this Learning Keepsake with me _____

Name of student   *Parent's/Guardian's signature*

MEET THE CHALLENGE

Strand 2 Topic 2
A TALK ON BEING HEALTHY

Learning outcome: 2.1

In pairs, write a talk you would give to First Year students on being healthy. Remember to:

○ introduce yourself to your audience and tell them why you are giving the talk

○ cover the important points about diet and exercise

○ use facts and statistics to support your points

○ include humour if you can

TOPIC 3
Substance Use

Why Use Drugs?

Learning outcome: 2.6

 responsible

 resilient

 aware

By the end of this lesson you will:

• understand what a drug is and the different types of drugs

• understand the damaging effects of drug use and misuse

KEYWORDS

Prescription
Over the counter
Addiction

USEFUL WEBSITE

www.drugs.ie Provides drug and alcohol information and support.

!!

A drug is any substance that changes the way the mind and/or body thinks, feels or behaves. Drugs are made from chemicals and they work by changing the chemistry of the body.

Expressing myself

CLASS ACTIVITY

Your teacher will read out the following statements regarding drugs and drug use. If you agree with the statement, raise your hand; if you disagree, raise both hands; and if you are unsure or undecided, keep both hands down.

Statements

Statements
All drugs are bad.
Medicines are a type of drug.
Drugs aren't bad, it's how we use them that can cause problems.
Prescription drugs are safer than illegal drugs.
Misuse of drugs can damage your mental health.
Some common household products can be just as dangerous as illegal drugs.
There should be no such thing as prescription drugs; all drugs should be available over the counter.

Learning with others

GROUP ACTIVITY

As a group, brainstorm all the different types of drugs that you have heard of.

Legal and illegal drugs

Drugs – legal and illegal – are used every day all over the world for a variety of purposes.

Legal drugs

Medicines

Some drugs are used to treat serious health conditions or diseases and can bring tremendous improvements and benefits to people's lives. These drugs are referred to as medicines.

- **Prescription medicines:** can only be given ('prescribed') by doctors, e.g. antibiotics.

- **Over-the-counter (OTC) medicines:** can be purchased in a pharmacy or shop, e.g. headache tablets.

It is important that only the person named on the prescription uses the medicine and that the doctor's directions or directions on the packaging are followed carefully.

There are strict rules around the manufacture and use of prescription and OTC drugs. Their content is known, controlled and always the same. These drugs are subject to a great deal of testing before they are approved. It is important that people do not misuse these drugs, as the consequences can be as harmful to a person's health and wellbeing as illegal drugs.

Socially acceptable drugs

Some drugs such as alcohol and nicotine (contained in cigarettes, e-cigarettes/vapes, etc.) are legal, which means they are available to be purchased by people over the legal age. The use of these drugs is governed for health and safety reasons as they are known to directly cause a great deal of harm to health when used or misused.

Caffeine, found in coffee, cola drinks and some energy drinks, can also come under this category. Misuse of caffeine (i.e. over-indulging in caffeine drinks) can cause irritability and restlessness, as well as affecting a person's sleep, which has knock-on effects on physical and mental wellbeing.

It is illegal to purchase alcohol or tobacco in Ireland if you are under eighteen.

Illegal drugs

Some drugs such as heroin, ecstasy and cannabis are illegal, which means there are laws in place that prevent us from using, buying or even being in possession of them. These laws are there to protect people from the harmful effects of these drugs. Not only can using these drugs have very damaging effects on our physical and mental health, being caught using or being in possession of them can result in a criminal conviction.

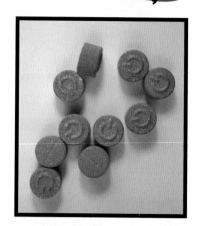

Solvents and other substances

Solvents and other substances such as aerosols, glue, etc. can be misused to get a chemical high. The use of such substances is extremely dangerous and can result in instant death.

Learning
with others

Review the list of drugs you brainstormed as a group. Write them under the appropriate headings in the table below. Add more if you can think of them now.

MEDICINES	SOCIALLY ACCEPTABLE	ILLEGAL	SOLVENTS/OTHER
paracetmal calpol	alchol vapes cigeverres caffiene	weed	

Drug addiction

Addiction occurs when a person becomes so dependent on a substance that they can no longer function without it. We often associate addiction and drug problems with illegal drugs such as heroin, but drug addiction and drug problems can also occur through the use of legal drugs such as alcohol, nicotine, prescription and OTC medicines. It can also occur through the misuse of solvents.

Misusing drugs in any way is harmful and can have serious consequences for a person's personal and social life, not to mention for their health and wellbeing. Young people may sometimes feel pressure to fit in, but it is important that we stay strong and resist pressures to abuse drugs of any kind. It's just not worth it. You can use some of the skills you learned in other areas of SPHE to help you cope with these pressures.

Co-operating and contributing

Learning creatively

CLASS ACTIVITY

As a class, create an anti-drug poster campaign that highlights the damaging effects of drug misuse. You can decide to focus on the dangers of misusing legal or illegal drugs, or solvent abuse, or a mixture of them all. (You might decide to split up into three groups with each group taking responsibility for one aspect of drug misuse.) Look at the examples below for inspiration, and then use all that you have learned to design your own anti-drug poster/s to display around your school.

LEARNING KEEPSAKE

Three things I have learned in this lesson are:

1. donr do drygs
2. donr vape
3. donr smoke

Something that helped me learn in this lesson was:

ms knightly

I could learn even better if:

_____ has shared this Learning Keepsake with me _____

Name of student   *Parent's/Guardian's signature*

LESSON 19

Smoking and its Effects

Learning outcomes: 2.5, 2.6

responsible

aware

By the end of this lesson you will:

→ have considered the health and social effects of smoking

→ have explored different techniques that help you resist the pressure to smoke

KEYWORDS

Lung cancer

Cardiovascular disease

USEFUL WEBSITES

www.quit.ie Dedicated to raising awareness about the dangers of smoking and provides advice and help for how to quit.

www.ash.ie Provides information about the dangers of smoking and e-cigarettes.

Being healthy   Making considered decisions

INDIVIDUAL ACTIVITY

Read this magazine article about smoking and answer the questions that follow.

How Smart is it to Smoke?

Answer: Not very!

The fact of the matter is, smoking is stupid. Plain and simple.

When you think of the physical action of what you are doing, it's pretty ridiculous, not to mention foul. You are taking smoky air into your lungs and then blowing it out. Would you run a tube up a smoky chimney and do the same? Would you stand right behind a bus and inhale the fumes? No!

116

It's not like anyone sets out to be a smoker. Sometimes it's curiosity, sometimes it's boredom, sometimes it's because all your friends are doing it. However, before you know what's happening, you're not just taking a cigarette from someone else, you're trying to buy a packet, or asking someone to buy you some (and think of the cost of them – €12 a pack!). Now it's not just when you're with your mates, it's when your parents aren't home and you're having a cheeky puff out the window. Next thing you know, you're craving another, you're addicted, and you're not even sure how much you like them.

A smoker is someone who smokes, and it doesn't have to be twenty a day. And being called a smoker is no compliment.

'How do I look?'

Before we even get started on the health risks, there are other smoking concerns to consider. Your physical appearance, for example. For a start, your teeth will turn a dull beige and eventually develop brown stains starting at the gums. Lovely!

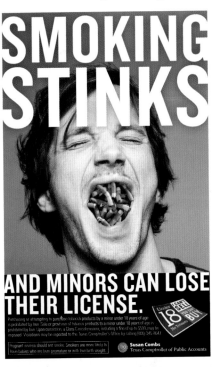

And not only that, your breath stinks. And we are not talking smoky-stinky, we're talking actual bad breath. Think of getting ready to go out, brushing your teeth, putting on some nice clean clothes, doing your hair – and out the door, only to light up a cigarette.

You might as well have not bothered. Hair, clothes, fingers … why waste your time getting ready when you're just going to ruin it by smelling awful? (And by the way, you might not be able to smell the cigarettes off yourself, but as soon as anyone else is around you after you've smoked, it's the first thing they'll smell, and it's gross.)

And if stinking to high heavens isn't bad enough, smoking actually causes premature ageing of the skin too. Now you may think this is no cause for concern right now, but you'll soon know all about it. Not only will it give you wrinkles around your eyes and forehead, you'll also get lovely wrinkles – 'smoker's lines', they're called – around your mouth. So while your non-smoking mates are enjoying getting ID'd by bouncers at the age of 28 ('Really? I look underage?'), you're getting asked for your pensioner's travel pass on the bus. Not good.

'What about my health?'

If brown teeth, stinky breath and premature wrinkles aren't enough to put you off smoking, then maybe the fact that it's the number one cause of lung cancer might convince you … not to mention the fact that your life will be shortened by ten to fifteen years, not to mention the yellow, sticky tar building up around your lungs, emphysema, bronchitis, strokes, heart disease, diabetes, cataracts … and not to mention the fact that if you were to buy one pack of cigarettes every week in Ireland for a year, you'd spend (lose) €624 annually. What a waste of money for something that not alone is of absolutely zero physical benefit, but actually actively harms you physically and socially. Doesn't really seem worth it.

1. 'Although young people are informed about the effects of smoking, they still do not regard it as dangerous.' Do you agree with this statement? Give reasons for your answer.

   _____

   _____

2. If you were trying to reduce smoking among young people in Ireland, what three facts about smoking would you consider the most important?

   (a) _____

   (b) _____

   (c) _____

3. What is your school's policy on smoking?

   _____

   _____

4. What do you think when you see anti-smoking campaigns, either on television or on billboards? Do you think they have any impact on a person's decision to smoke?

   _____

   _____

5. Write a health warning on this box of cigarettes that you think would encourage young people to quit smoking.

What causes the damage?

Tobacco is a toxic substance that contains the highly addictive substance nicotine. Along with tobacco, cigarettes contain around 7,000 additional chemicals, including arsenic (which is also used in rat poison) and acetone (also used in nail polish remover). Many of these chemicals are poisonous and over sixty are known to be cancer-causing (carcinogenic).

What about passive smoking?

Passive smoking means breathing in other people's exhaled smoke. Exhaled smoke is called mainstream smoke. The smoke drifting from a lit cigarette is called sidestream smoke. Sidestream smoke is four times more toxic than mainstream smoke because it is not filtered. It also contains three times as much carbon monoxide. A child exposed to this second-hand smoke (or 'environmental tobacco') is more likely to develop symptoms of asthma.

You probably find if you're sitting in a room where people are smoking that you experience a sore throat, itchy, runny eyes, coughing, sneezing and headache. It may also make you feel nauseous, dizzy or even cause respiratory problems such as bronchitis or pneumonia.

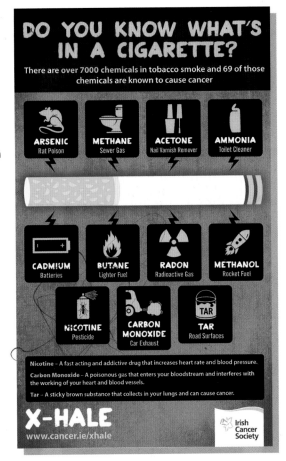

(Source: www.cancer.ie)

Some facts about smoking

- Smoking is the single biggest killer of people in Ireland, accounting for some 5,500 deaths every year.

- Every 6.5 seconds, someone in the world dies because of their tobacco use.

- Every cigarette a person smokes reduces his/her life by 5.5 minutes.

- One in two smokers will die from a tobacco-related illness such as cancer, heart disease, lung disease, cardiovascular disease and exacerbation of diabetes.

- One cigar can contain as much tobacco as a pack of cigarettes.

- Smoking does not relax you – it triggers stress.

- It takes twenty minutes for a smoker's pulse rate to return to normal after having a cigarette.

- Smoking can affect a person's physical fitness. Muscles need oxygen to perform and the carbon monoxide in cigarettes deprives the muscles of oxygen and causes shortness of breath.

- Smoking while pregnant damages the unborn child. It can cause low birth weight and it increases the risk of premature birth or dying after birth.

- Most smokers (83%) regret that they ever started smoking.

- Smoking twenty cigarettes a day could cost a person over €4,300 a year.
- It is illegal for anyone under the age of eighteen to buy cigarettes in Ireland.
- Young people most commonly start smoking because their friends smoke.
- The benefits of quitting smoking are felt almost immediately by the body.

I will never smoke because _____.

Dangers of smoking crossword

Across

3 The feeling a person gets that makes them want to smoke another cigarette.

5 One of the 7,000 chemicals used in cigarettes, also used in rat poison.

7 Cancer caused by smoking.

9 Sticky, yellow substance that builds up in the lungs.

12 Gas that robs the body of oxygen and causes shortness of breath.

13 Out of 100 people who smoke, the number of people who will die of a smoking-related illness.

Down

1 The number of minutes it takes for a smoker's heart to return to normal after smoking a cigarette.

2 This type of smoking harms non-smokers.

4 The reason why people find it is hard to give up smoking.

6 Visible signs of premature ageing caused by smoking.

8 The main addictive ingredient in cigarettes.

10 The benefits of this are felt almost immediately by the body.

11 The most common reason why young people start smoking.

HOW TO SAY NO TO SMOKING

Saying no to cigarettes can be tough but it's worth the effort for your health, your pocket, the planet and everyone around you. Here's some tips on what to do and say if you're ever put under pressure to smoke...

WHAT TO DO

Stand tall, hold your head high and speak with confidence

Remind yourself of the risks of smoking and why you're saying no

Remember that you don't need to smoke to be cool or fit in, real friends like you for who you are

Walk away if you feel uncomfortable

HELP Don't suffer in silence or give in, talk to someone you trust if you're feeling under pressure

WHAT TO SAY

I don't smoke

It's not my style

I don't want my clothes, hair and breath to stink, it's disgusting!

NO THANKS..

Wrinkles, yellow teeth and brown fingers are not a good look

I like to be active, wheezing lungs hold you back

I can think of better things to do with my cash

X-HALE
www.cancer.ie/xhale

Irish Cancer Society

(Source: www.cancer.ie)

LEARNING KEEPSAKE

Three things I have learned in this lesson are:

1. _____

2. _____

3. _____

Something that helped me learn in this lesson was:

_____

_____

_____

I could have learned better if:

_____

_____

_____

_____ has shared this Learning Keepsake with me _____

Name of student   *Parent's/Guardian's signature*

LESSON 20

Alcohol: The Facts

Learning outcomes: 2.5, 2.6, 4.7

responsible connected aware

By the end of this lesson you will:

→ understand how alcohol affects personal health, wellbeing and relationships

→ demonstrate the skills to resist the pressure to drink alcohol

KEYWORDS

Standard drink

Alcohol limit

USEFUL WEBSITES

www.drugs.ie Provides drug and alcohol information and support.

www.drinkaware.ie Provides facts on alcohol use in Ireland.

www.barnardos.ie/resources/young-people/drugs-alcohol Provides support and resources for young people experiencing issues with alcohol themselves or in the home.

www.askaboutalcohol.ie Provides support and advice on alcohol use for individuals or families experiencing alcohol issues.

Alcohol plays a very big part in Irish culture and social life. We are exposed to alcohol from many different angles: through TV adverts, sport sponsorship or generally accepted ideas on the role of alcohol in any type of social situation, from baptisms to funerals.

Being healthy
and safe

As a group, read these statements and tick which ones are myths, which ones are fact and which ones you are unsure about. Discuss the reasons for each choice. You will discuss the statements as a class afterwards.

STATEMENT	MYTH	FACT	UNSURE
1. Alcohol works to cheer people up.			
2. Drinking coffee or taking a cold shower after drinking helps sober a person up.			
3. Mixing alcohol with energy drinks is potentially dangerous.			
4. It is ok to have one drink and drive.			
5. In Ireland, it is against the law to sell alcohol to anyone under eighteen.			
6. Alcohol is a contributory factor in over 1,000 deaths a year in Ireland, or three deaths on average a day.			
7. Alcohol can lead to risky behaviour.			
8. More than one in four of people who have to go to Accident & Emergency have alcohol-related injuries.			
9. Too much alcohol can poison a person's body.			
10. Every day, 500 beds in our hospitals are occupied by people with alcohol-related problems.			
11. Eating while drinking slows down the absorption of alcohol.			
12. Women and men can drink the same amount of alcohol, with the same effects.			

Facts about alcohol

Alcohol increases the risk of road accidents

Alcohol is involved in two in every five fatal road collisions. A person who drinks and drives does not just put themselves at risk but also their passengers, other drivers and road-users, and pedestrians. The introduction of random breath testing and the lowering of the drink-driving limits have improved road safety. The Road Safety Authority's advice is **never ever drink and drive**.

Drinking during adolescence can cause brain damage

The human brain continues to develop during adolescence and is not considered fully developed until a person reaches their mid-twenties. This means that during adolescence, the brain is much more at risk to damage from alcohol. Drinking alcohol while the brain is still developing damages two key parts of the brain: the part responsible for logic, reasoning, self-regulation and judgement, and the part responsible for learning and memory. This damage can be long-term and irreversible.

Alcohol can cause mental health problems

Alcohol is a depressant. After drinking alcohol, a person can feel low or down. In the long term, alcohol use can cause depression, anxiety and stress. Drinking alcohol can prevent young people developing the coping skills and resilience that contribute to positive mental health in later life. As well as that, when a person drinks too much they can lose their inhibitions, which can greatly increase the chances of them getting into embarrassing situations at best, or risky or dangerous situations at worst. All these factors can seriously impact on a young person's mental health.

Starting drinking early in life increases your risk of becoming dependent

Evidence shows that young people who start drinking in their early teens are more likely to become addicted.

Alcohol affects sports performance

If you are serious about athletics or playing sports, then alcohol is a no-go area. Alcohol affects endurance, muscle development and recovery. It affects the ability of muscles to absorb the nutrients they need to work properly. Playing sports with a hangover increases the risk of cramp and affects coordination, reaction time and balance. Alcohol can also reduce B vitamins, which help repair the body after injury, and testosterone in males, which is needed for muscle development.

GLASS OF PROSECCO 12% (150ml)	CAN OF CIDER 4.5% (500ml x 6 pack)
114 calories 2 grams sugar Half teaspoon	1,260 calories 126 grams sugar 25 teaspoons
BOTTLE OF WHITE WINE 12.5% (750ml)	SPIRIT AND SOFT DRINK 35.5ml (of spirits)
564 calories 22.5 grams sugar 4.5 teaspoons	163 calories 21 grams sugar 4 teaspoons
ALCOPOP 4% (250ml x 4 pack)	BOTTLE OF WHITE WINE 14% (750ml)
527 calories 88 grams sugar 18 teaspoons	720 calories 44 grams sugar 9 teaspoons
PINT OF LAGER 3% (568ml)	BOTTLE OF RED WINE 12.5% (750ml)
91 calories 3 grams sugar Half teaspoon	570 calories 11 grams sugar 2 teaspoons
QUARTER BOTTLE OF WHITE WINE 12.5% (187.5ml)	IRISH CREAM LIQUEUR 17% (50ml)
141 calories 6 grams sugar 1 teaspoon	18 calories 10 grams sugar 2 teaspoons

Drinking alcohol can lead to obesity

Alcohol is high in calories and contains a lot of sugar. These calories are known as 'empty calories' because they have no nutritional value. One standard drink can contain over 200 calories. As well as that, drinking alcohol gives a false appetite, which contributes to poor eating choices, for example getting a takeaway after a night out.

Drinking while pregnant affects the unborn child

Drinking alcohol while pregnant can affect the foetus with a range of conditions known as foetal alcohol spectrum disorder, including reduced birth weight and hearing and sight issues. Even moderate drinking increases the risk of miscarriage or stillbirth. Women are also advised not to drink if breastfeeding their baby.

Problem drinking in the home

Many young people in Ireland are affected by the drinking habits of their parents/guardians. It can be a big worry for a young person if a parent or guardian is drinking too much. It is important to remember the 'Seven Cs' in realising that problem drinking is not the fault of the child.

- You didn't cause it.

- You cannot cure it.

- You cannot control it.

- You can care for yourself.

- You can communicate your feelings.

- You can make healthy choices.

- You can celebrate yourself.

(Source: www.barnardos.ie)

If you are affected by another person's drinking, it is important to talk to a trusted adult. This could be someone in your family like an aunt, uncle or grandparent. You could also talk to someone outside your family, for example a school counsellor. The 'how to get help' section of these websites can provide you with details of support services: www.barnardos.ie/teenhelp and **www.askaboutalcohol.ie.**

Standard drinks and binge drinking

A 'standard drink' is a measure of alcohol, and how it is measured out depends on the strength of the alcohol (shown on the label as alcohol by volume or % ABV – so, for example, 5% ABV means 5 parts alcohol to 95 parts water). Binge drinking is when six or more standard drinks are consumed in one sitting (for example, three pints of 4.5% beer).

A STANDARD DRINK IS

Half pint of lager, beer or stout (284ml)   Small glass of wine (284ml)   Pub measure of spirit (35.5ml)

Drinks should be spaced out over the week and should never be saved up to drink on one occasion. The low-risk drinking guidelines displayed in the infographic are for adults only (there is no safe limit of drinking for anyone drinking illegally under the age of eighteen), but it is important to note that health authorities now advise that there is no 'safe' level of alcohol intake regardless of whether the person drinking is an adult or an adolescent.

Low-risk drinking guidelines

UP TO **17** STANDARD DRINKS SPREAD OUT OVER ONE WEEK

UP TO **11** STANDARD DRINKS SPREAD OUT OVER ONE WEEK

At least two alcohol-free days per week for both

INDIVIDUAL ACTIVITY

Evaluating information

From what you have read so far, write down one fact that surprised you and explain why.

Fact that surprised me: _____

Why? _____

_____

_____

_____

 # CLASS DISCUSSION

Discussing/Debating

Can you think of situations where drinking alcohol can lead to risky behaviour for young people?

What are these risks?

Who can young people talk to if they feel they have a problem with alcohol, or if they are being affected by alcohol in the home?

How alcohol affects different parts of the body

The moment alcohol enters your system, it starts affecting your body and mind. Alcohol passes through the body from the mouth to the stomach into the circulatory system, the brain, the kidneys, lungs and liver.

Brain

Alcohol affects the part of the brain that is responsible for self-control. As a person drinks, their reactions, vision and judgement become impaired. The more a person drinks, the harder basic tasks – such as walking and talking – become. After drinking, people sometimes behave out of character, doing things they don't mean to or wouldn't if they were sober. An excessive amount of alcohol in the body can result in coma, brain damage and even death.

Liver

Ninety per cent of alcohol is broken down by the liver, but the liver can only deal with one drink per hour. Alcohol damages the liver when it is consumed regularly.

Kidneys

Alcohol stimulates urine production, which causes a person to urinate more. This leads to dehydration.

Circulatory system

Once it is in the bloodstream, alcohol is distributed around the body. Alcohol causes the blood vessels to widen, which causes flushed skin and increased body temperature.

Stomach

Alcohol passes through the walls of the stomach and small intestines into the bloodstream. If the stomach is empty the alcohol passes straight through; if the stomach has food in it, the alcohol is absorbed more slowly. Alcohol stimulates the stomach juices, which causes an increase in appetite.

Speech

Too much alcohol can affect the way a person speaks, as well as what they say. It can cause slurred speech. It can also cause people to say things they wouldn't normally.

Skin

Drinking alcohol dehydrates the skin, causing bloating and dark circles under the eyes.

Lungs

Alcohol in its gaseous state is inhaled into the bloodstream and goes straight to the lungs.

INDIVIDUAL ACTIVITY

Learning creatively

Your class are going to take part in a T-shirt campaign to help young people resist the pressure to drink alcohol. Design a T-shirt that gives practical tips on how to say no to alcohol. For example:

YOU DON'T NEED TO DRINK ALCOHOL TO FIT IN – REAL FRIENDS LIKE YOU FOR WHO YOU ARE!

YOU DON'T NEED DRINK TO HAVE FUN!

THINK BEFORE YOU DRINK!

A catchy slogan could be a great way to get your message across.

LEARNING KEEPSAKE

Three things I have learned in this lesson are:

1. _____
2. _____
3. _____

Something that helped me learn in this lesson was:

_____

_____

_____

I could learn even better if:

_____

_____

_____

_____ has shared this Learning Keepsake with me _____

Name of student   *Parent's/Guardian's signature*

TOPIC 4
Anti-Bullying

Dealing with Bullying: What Can You Do?

Learning outcomes: 2.9, 2.10

 responsible resilient respected connected aware

By the end of this lesson you will:

» understand what bullying is

» be able to identify different types of bullying behaviour

» describe appropriate responses to incidences of bullying

KEYWORDS

Policy

Strategies

Bystander

USEFUL WEBSITES

www.childline.ie A 24-hour helpline and online service offering information and support for young people and teenagers experiencing bullying and other issues. **Freephone 1800 666 666.**

www.teenline.ie Helpline and online service offering information and support for teenagers experiencing bullying and other issues. **Freephone 1800 833 634**.

www.kidshealth.org Offers information on bullying and related topics.

www.belongto.org Offers support and advice for lesbian, gay, bisexual and transgender young people.

Bullying is when someone is hurt physically or emotionally, either by words or actions, on purpose. Posting something hurtful about someone online, even once, is regarded as bullying. This is because once something goes online, it can go viral – it can be viewed, copied or forwarded for many people to see.

INDIVIDUAL ACTIVITY

Being safe

There are many different types of bullying. Match the type of bullying to the correct description by writing the letter of the type of bullying in the box beside its description..

TYPE OF BULLYING
A. Physical bullying
B. Exclusion bullying
C. Cyberbullying
D. Gesture bullying
E. Relational bullying
F. Verbal bullying
G. Identity-based bullying
H. Extortion bullying

DESCRIPTION	
1. Involves saying nasty things to hurt other people's feelings, e.g. about their sexuality, appearance, clothes, ethnicity, family.	f
2. Threatening to hurt a person to force them to hand over money, or to do something they don't want to do. Can often happen online.	e
3. Often takes place in friend groups and involves trying to make someone feel bad by, e.g., eye-rolling, whispering, passing notes, mimicking, laughing behind someone's back with other group members. Less easy to pinpoint than physical bullying and can go unnoticed for a long time. Difficult to describe and report especially because the person acting this way can often seem friendly in other situations.	b
4. Involves actions such as: kicking, tripping, hair-pulling, punching, spitting, poking, fighting, etc. It can also involve damaging a person's property, e.g. books, clothes, etc.	A
5. Involves threatening body language and non-verbal signs to intimidate another person.	D
6. Targeted at a person because of their actual or perceived identity group such as: sexual orientation, gender identity, disability, ethnicity, religion, immigration status, etc.	G
7. Using information technology and social media to bully someone online. Takes the form of threatening or hurtful messages by email, text, or posting on social media sites.	C
8. Where a person is deliberately ignored and/or left out of conversations, activities and online groups to make them feel isolated.	H

INDIVIDUAL ACTIVITY

Being safe/Reading with
critical understanding

Read the following scenarios and answer the questions that follow them.

The Text Message

John and his friends are sitting on the wall outside the local shop on a Sunday evening. They see Laura, a girl from school, coming out of the shop. Laura is a well-liked girl but she is not one of the popular group. John has heard that she fancies his best friend, Mark, and seeing her, has a great idea for a laugh. He asks his friends if either of them has Laura's mobile number. Luke has it because he is in the same athletics club as Laura.

John texts Laura, pretending to be Mark. 'Hi Laura, Mark here, what's up?' Laura replies, 'Not much, just hanging around at home a bit bored'. John texts back, 'I really like you and I'd love to go out with you.' Laura is delighted and texts back, 'I really like you too. When would you like to meet?'

John doesn't respond but instead forwards the texts to all of the lads and some of the girls from school.

The next day, when Laura comes into school, she sees some of the girls in her class seemingly talking about her and laughing. Laura's friend, Jean, comes up to her and tells Laura about the text and says that she got it from John on Sunday night. Jean also says that some people are even laughing about it on Facebook. Their teacher comes into the classroom, and noticing that some of the class are laughing and Laura is looking upset, tells them all to sit down and gives Laura a sympathetic smile.

1. What type/s of bullying did Laura experience?

    _____

    _____

    _____

2. Describe how Laura must be feeling after hearing from her friend what everyone is laughing about. Name as many emotions as you can.

    _____

    _____

    _____

3. Who could have helped Laura and what could they have done?

    _____

    _____

    _____

4. Why do you think Mark decided to behave as he did? Is Mark the only bully in this story?

    _____

    _____

    _____

The Football Game

Danny is in First Year in school. He is very outspoken and often talks out of turn in class. Danny doesn't mean to be cheeky, but he is very interested in lots of different subjects and likes to discuss things with his teachers. Lately, Danny has noticed that some of the other students start sniggering when he talks. In particular, two boys from his primary school, Conor and Jack, make fun of Danny whenever he says anything.

Danny is quite good at soccer and he plays with the school team. One day after losing a match, Danny and the rest of the team are getting changed in the changing rooms. Conor and Jack are on the team too, and they are not happy that they lost. They blame Danny for losing the match, saying that he did not mark his man properly. Danny tries to ignore them and continues to get changed. Then Conor shouts that they will never win anything with a gay person on the team. He goes over to Danny and pushes him. Danny falls backwards and lands on the floor and Conor starts kicking him. Everyone else in the dressing room starts to shout, 'Fight, fight, fight!' and some of the team take out their phones to record it.

Eventually the coach comes in and stops the fight. He tries to find out what happened but no one is willing to tell him. The school is holding an investigation into what happened. Meanwhile, Danny can't face his team, or going to school.

1. What type/s of bullying did Danny experience?

   _____

   _____

   _____

2. Describe how Danny must have felt after he was beaten up in the changing room and the event was recorded. Describe as many emotions as you can.

   _____

   _____

   _____

3. Do you think this type of bullying is typical among boys?

   _____

   _____

   _____

4. Is there anyone who could have helped Danny? How could they have helped?

   _____

   _____

   _____

Tips for dealing with bullying

☞ **Try speaking to the bully.** If you feel safe and comfortable doing so, try to speak to the bully about how their behaviour is making you feel. You may ask them why they are doing this to you. When telling the bully how their behaviour is affecting you, use 'I' statements, e.g.'I feel … when you …' Try to make sure that other people are around when you confront the bully. If confronting the bully is too difficult, then don't.

☞ **Use positive self-talk.** Tell yourself that you do not deserve to be treated this way and that what the bully is saying is not true.

☞ **Ignore it.** Try to ignore the behaviour and try not to show that you are upset. This is hard, but bullies thrive on other people's reactions and/or fears. If they don't get a reaction, they may give up.

☞ **Walk away from the situation.** Try to walk away from the situation. Try not to fight back or use violence. This can only make things worse.

☞ **Use humour.** Try to use humour to lighten the mood if the situation allows.

☞ **Get support from your friends.** Try to make sure that you do not become isolated in the presence of the bully. Try to get support from your friends. If your group of friends are responsible for the bullying, you need to consider leaving that friend group and making new friends.

☞ **Tell a trusted adult.** If you find that you cannot turn to friends or deal with the bullying yourself, you need to tell a trusted adult. If the bullying is serious, it needs to be reported to the school.

Could you be a bully?

These questions will help you to reflect on your own behaviour.

(a) Have you ever hurt someone on purpose?

(b) Have you ever deliberately tried to make someone else feel bad by saying something hurtful, or knowingly excluding them from a situation?

(c) Have you ever picked on someone younger than you?

(d) Do you spread rumours knowing that they are not true?

(e) Have you tried to turn your friends against someone?

(f) Have you ever laughed along with a bully?

(g) Have you ever used the excuse that you were only messing when you know that you were not?

If answering these questions has made you feel uneasy, then you need to think about how you treat others. If you are bullying someone, you can stop by doing the following:

- Apologise to the person face to face or write them an apology letter.
- Repair the damage done by removing insulting pictures or harmful messages.
- Talk to a parent or teacher about what you have done and seek advice on how to rectify the situation.

Why do you behave this way?

- Why do you feel the need to pick on other people?
- Have you been or are you being bullied, and are you angry about this?
- Do you make someone else feel small to make yourself feel better?
- Is there something you enjoy about making someone else feel bad? If so, why? Is it fair?
- Do you think your behaviour makes you look and feel powerful?

If you answer yes to any of these statements, then you need to face up to what you are doing and talk to a trusted adult for advice.

INDIVIDUAL ACTIVITY

Writing   Learning creatively

Imagine you are an agony aunt/uncle at a magazine for young people. Laura or Danny have written you a letter about the bullying situation they find themselves in. Write a letter to them giving them advice on what to do and how to deal and cope with their situation.

TEEN LIFE ADVICE

Dear

_____   _____

_____   _____

_____   _____

_____   _____

_____   _____

_____   _____

_____   _____

_____   _____

Learning Keepsake

Three things I have learned in this lesson are:

1. _____

2. _____

3. _____

Something that helped me learn in this lesson was:

_____

_____

_____

I could learn even better if:

_____

_____

_____

_____ has shared this Learning Keepsake with me _____

Name of student   *Parent's/Guardian's signature*

LESSON 22

Bullying is Everyone's Business

responsible   connected   resilient   respected   aware

Learning outcomes: 2.9, 2.10, 2.11

By the end of this lesson you will:

➜ have looked at the roles of participants and bystanders in incidents of bullying

KEYWORDS

Participants

Bystanders

USEFUL WEBSITES

www.childline.ie A 24-hour helpline and online service offering information and support for young people and teenagers experiencing bullying and other issues. **Freephone 1800 666 666.**

www.teenline.ie Helpline and online service offering information and support for teenagers experiencing bullying and other issues. **Freephone 1800 833 634.**

www.kidshealth.org Offers information on bullying and related topics.

www.belongto.org Offers support and advice for lesbian, gay, bisexual and transgender young people.

Bullying can severely affect a person's self-esteem and self-confidence. The bullied person may feel isolated and withdraw from their friends and peers.

CLASS ACTIVITY

Listening and expressing myself

Brainstorm as many words as possible that show how bullying affects a person.

INDIVIDUAL ACTIVITY

Learning creatively

Making the world a better place

Read the following poem taken from an anti-bullying campaign and try to fill in what you think are the missing words. When you have done that, you might like to look up 'I Am Anti-Bullying Campaign advert' on YouTube to see various famous people recite this poem. See if you got the words right. Then answer the questions that follow.

I AM

by Laura

I am the person you bullied at school,

I am the person who didn't know how to __ _____

I am the person you alienated,

I am the person you ridiculed and _____.

I am the person who sat on her own,

I am the person who walked _____ _____,

I am the person you _____ every day,

I am the person who had nothing to ____.

I am the person with hurt in her _____,

I am the person you never saw cry,

I am the person living alone with her fears,

I am the person destroyed by ____ _____.

I am the person who drowned in your scorn,

I am the person who wished she hadn't been _____,

I am the person you destroyed for 'fun',

I am the person, but not the only ____.

I am the person whose name you don't know,

I am the person who just can't let ___,

I am the person who has feelings too,

And I was a person, _____ _____ ___.

1. How did this poem make you feel?_____

2. How does the poem make you feel about the person being bullied?

   _____

3. How do you think the person being bullied feels?

   _____

4. What are your feelings towards the bully?

   _____

5. How do you think the bully would feel after reading this poem?

   _____

6. What advice would you give to this person if you knew them?

   _____

7. What advice would you give to the bully?

The role of the bystander

Bystanders are onlookers who witness bullying behaviour. They are not the targets or the recipients of the bully's words or actions. Bystanders can have a role in stopping bullying behaviour. The picture below shows how different bystanders can be participants and/or witnesses to bullying.

1 Bullies: start the bullying and take an active part in it.

3 Reinforcers: take an active part but do not start the bullying.

5 Passive supporters: support the bullying behaviour but do not show support.

7 Resisters: dislike the bullying and try to help.

2 Target: the one who is being bullied.

4 Disengaged onlookers: watch what is happening but don't take a stand, taking the view that it's none of their business.

6 Unsure witnesses: Dislike the bullying and think they should help but don't do anything/ don't know what to do.

CLASS DISCUSSION

Discussing/Debating

Some studies have shown that when bystanders take action, bullying can stop within ten seconds.

How does each bystander influence the outcome of the bullying situation?

What might prevent someone from taking action or intervening to stop bullying?

How can bystanders play an important role in stopping bullying without putting themselves in danger?

Learning creatively

INDIVIDUAL ACTIVITY

Using the poem 'I Am' as an example, write two verses of a positive poem about the person who stops to help. The poem has been started for you

I am the person who stopped the fight

I am the person who knew it wasn't right

I am the person who _____

I am the person who _____

I am the person who _____

I am the person who _____

I am the person who _____

And I am the person who _____

LEARNING KEEPSAKE

Three things I have learned in this lesson are:

1. _____

2. _____

3. _____

Something that helped me learn in this lesson was:

_____

_____

_____

I could learn even better if:

_____

_____

_____

_____ has shared this Learning Keepsake with me _____

Name of student   *Parent's/Guardian's signature*

MEET THE CHALLENGE

Strand 2 Topic 4

'TAKE A STAND AGAINST BULLYING' POSTER CAMPAIGN

Learning outcome: 2.11

Create a poster campaign that encourages people to take a stand against bullying. When deciding what text to put on your poster:

○ create a catchy slogan (you can work off the 'Take a Stand' idea, e.g. Stand up to/Stand up against/Stand strong against, etc.)

○ include advice about who can support young people if they witness bullying

○ remind people about respectful and assertive communication

○ remind people not to put themselves in danger and to stay safe

When making your poster:

○ consider where you will be hanging your poster

○ choose one large visual to represent your idea

○ use large typography (writing) so your message is clear and can be seen from a distance

○ use colour in an interesting way, e.g. contrast/black and white, etc.

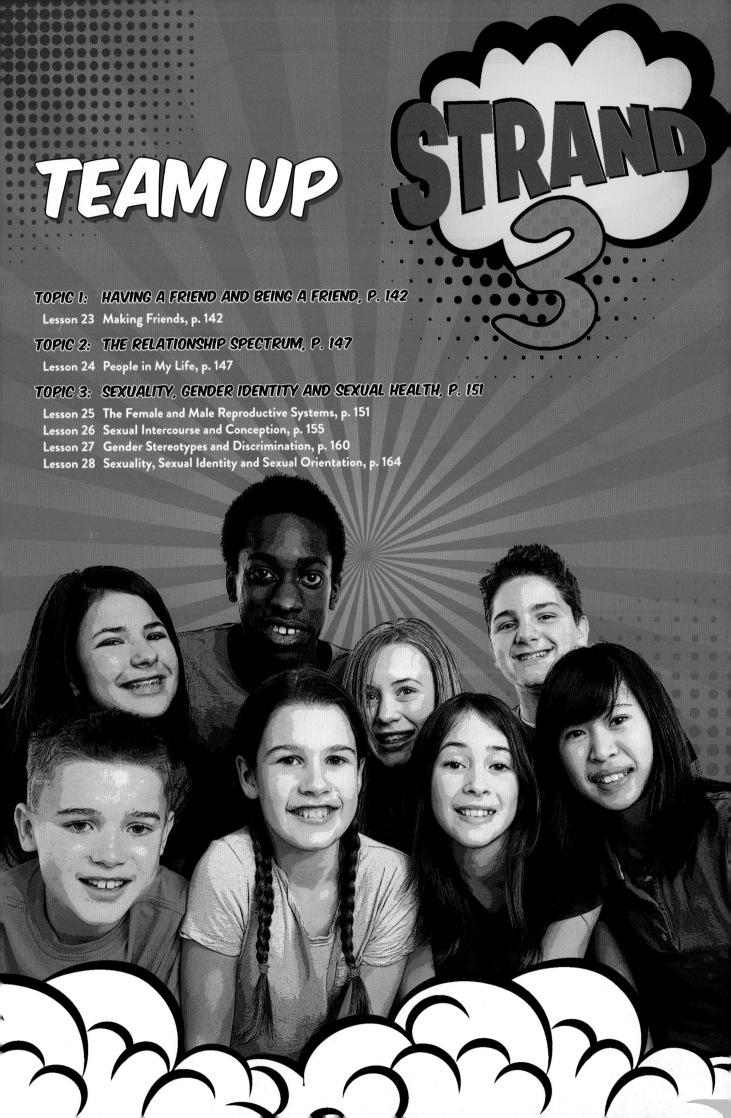

TEAM UP

STRAND 3

TOPIC 1
Having a Friend and Being a Friend

LESSON 23

Making Friends

Learning outcomes: 3.2, 3.3

 responsible
 connected
 resilient
 respected
 aware

By the end of this lesson you will:
- know how to make and maintain friendships
- recognise what makes a good friend
- recognise what makes you a good friend

KEYWORD

Friendship

USEFUL WEBSITES

www.kidshealth.org Search 'good friends' for information on friendship and relationships.

www.cyh.com Go to the 'Friends' section for useful tips on making and keeping friends.

INDIVIDUAL ACTIVITY

Knowing myself

In order to make good friends, it is important for you to know the qualities you value in a person. Look at these statements about what a friend might be and rank them in order of how important they are to you from 1–9, with 1 being the least important and 9 being the most important to you.

A FRIEND IS	RANK
Someone who is good fun	
Someone who can keep secrets	
Someone who stands up for you	
Someone who gives you compliments	
Someone who is popular	
Someone who accepts you the way you are	
Someone who buys you things	
Someone who makes you laugh	
Someone who is intelligent	

GROUP ACTIVITY

Co-operating Discussing/ Debating

As a group, agree on nine qualities of a friend that you think are important (you may come up with new ones in addition to the list above). In the diamond, rank how important your group thinks each quality is by writing what you consider to be the least important at the bottom, working your way up to the top for what you consider to be the most important quality.

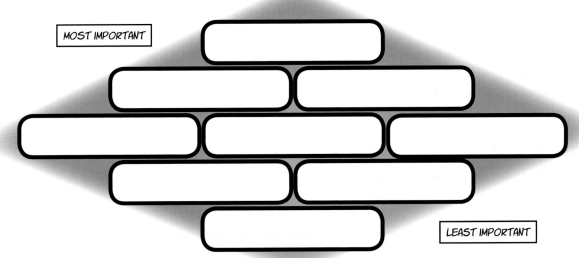

MOST IMPORTANT

LEAST IMPORTANT

CLASS DISCUSSION

Discussing/Debating

INDIVIDUAL ACTIVITY

Knowing myself

Answer these questions:

1. Do all your friends have all the qualities you like or admire in a friend?

_____

_____

2. What is the difference between a friend in real life and a friend on the internet?

_____

_____

Tips for making and keeping friends

☞ Be yourself. Do not pretend to be someone you're not. This never works, and people see through it.

☞ Be open and don't be afraid to share your opinions and feelings.

☞ Treat your friend the way you would like to be treated.

☞ Don't talk about your friends behind their back.

☞ Listen to others and don't always be talking about yourself.

☞ Have empathy. This means putting yourself in your friend's shoes to understand where they are coming from.

☞ Be kind and do nice things for your friend.

☞ Accept your friends for who they are and don't try to change them.

☞ If there are arguments or disagreements, sit down and listen to each other's side of things.

☞ Don't pressurise your friends into doing things they are not comfortable with. Accept their decisions.

INDIVIDUAL ACTIVITY

Knowing myself

Write five qualities you have as a friend into the fingers of the hand outline. Write a quality you could improve on into the palm.

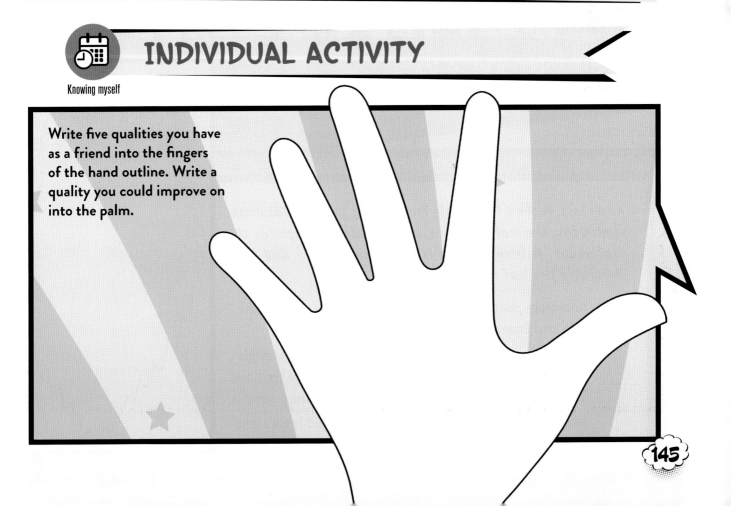

LEARNING KEEPSAKE

Three things I have learned in this lesson are:

1. _____
2. _____
3. _____

Something that helped me learn in this lesson was:

_____

_____

_____

I could learn even better if:

_____

_____

_____

_____ has shared this Learning Keepsake with me _____

Name of student   *Parent's/Guardian's signature*

MEET THE CHALLENGE

Strand 3 Topic 1
MAKING A FRIENDSHIP TREE

Learning outcome: 3.1

As a class, make a Friendship Tree to hang on your classroom wall. Using the leaf template, every student completes the statement 'A friend to me is someone who ...' and then decorates the leaf for sticking on the tree.

○ Designate people who will draw, colour and cut out the tree and branches base for your leaves.

○ Designate people who will collect the correct materials for completing the task, e.g. paper (to draw the tree and branches base), pencils, scissors, glue, colouring pencils.

○ Designate students to collect the completed leaves and stick them on the tree.

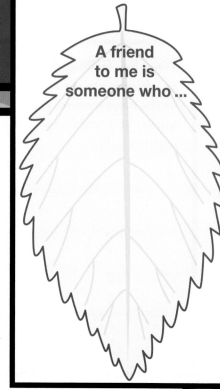

A friend to me is someone who ...

TOPIC 2
The Relationship Spectrum

People in My Life

Learning outcome: 3.4

responsible   aware

By the end of this lesson you will:

→ be more aware of the people who influence you

→ have examined how and why people influence you

KEYWORDS

Influences

Decisions

Have you ever asked yourself the question, 'Who influences me?' Probably not, because a lot of the time we are unaware of the influence other people have on us.

Each day people influence the decisions we make. A family member or teacher may influence the career path you take; the latest fashions may influence what you wear; an advertisement may persuade you to buy a particular product.

147

INDIVIDUAL ACTIVITY

Knowing myself

1. Using the pictures as prompts, think of the different ways in which people such as these can influence someone your age.

SPORTSPEOPLE

PARENTS/CAREGIVERS

CELEBRITIES

FRIENDS

TEACHERS

POLITICIANS

2. On the stairs, rank how influential you think these categories of people are in the life of a young person. Place the category with the least influence on the first step, all the way up to the category with the most influence on the top step, in your opinion. To the side of the steps, in the spaces provided, write a note on how each category might influence the lives of young people.

CLASS DISCUSSION

Discussing/Debating

Who is the biggest influence in your life?

How does this person influence you?

INDIVIDUAL ACTIVITY

Writing

Write a letter to the person who is the biggest influence in your life. In your letter, let the person know what talents and/or qualities they have that influence you so much. Tell them also how their influence affects your everyday life. Ask them what their own influences were, and finish up by thanking them.

Dear

_____

_____

_____

_____

_____

_____

_____

_____

_____

_____

Yours sincerely,

_____

LEARNING KEEPSAKE

Three things I have learned in this lesson are:

1. _____

2. _____

3. _____

Something that helped me learn in this lesson was:

_____

_____

_____

I could learn even better if:

_____

_____

_____

_____ has shared this Learning Keepsake with me _____

Name of student   *Parent's/Guardian's signature*

TOPIC 3
Sexuality, Gender Identity and Sexual Health

The Female and Male Reproductive Systems

Learning outcome: 3.6

responsible   aware

By the end of this lesson you will:

•▸ have a clear understanding of the male and female reproductive systems

KEYWORD

Reproductive system

USEFUL WEBSITE

www.kidshealth.org Contains informative animations on the male and female reproductive systems.

You will have learned about the male and female reproductive systems in SPHE class in primary school. Like all living things, human beings reproduce. The male and female reproductive organs work together to produce a baby. Let's see how much you remember.

INDIVIDUAL ACTIVITY

Gathering data

1. Look at the diagram of the female reproductive system. Match each part with its correct description by writing the correct number in the box beside the description.

Part of female reproductive system	Number in diagram
Ovaries: Organs where eggs/ovum (the female reproductive cell) are produced, one on either side of uterus.	
Uterus (womb): Where the foetus grows during pregnancy. A hollow, pear-shaped organ with a hollow wall. Lining (endometrium) released from body during menstruation.	
Fallopian tubes: Join uterus to ovaries. During ovulation, egg released into these.	
Cervix: Lower part of uterus/neck of womb that opens into vagina. During childbirth, can expand about 10 cm to allow baby to travel from uterus through vagina and out of mother's body.	
Vagina: Hollow muscular tube connecting uterus to outside of body. Entrance to vagina is outside the body.	

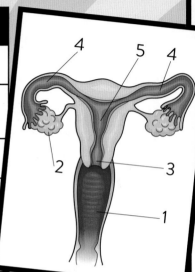

2. Look at the diagram of the male reproductive system. Match each part with its correct description by writing the correct number in the box beside the description.

Part of male reproductive system	Number in diagram
Bladder: Muscular sac that stores urine until released from urethra.	
Prostate gland: Walnut-sized gland surrounding portion of urethra. Produces some of the fluid in semen.	
Vas deferens: Thin, muscular tube that carries sperm to urethra.	
Urethra: Tube that carries urine and semen outside of penis. Urine and semen cannot leave at same time. When penis is ready to release semen, a valve blocks off bladder so urine cannot leave.	
Foreskin: Loose skin that covers shaft and glans of the penis. Can be pulled back gently allowing penis to be washed and kept clean. Some males have foreskin removed (circumcision). Circumcision does not affect function of penis.	
Scrotum: Sac holding testicles that keeps them at proper temperature to produce healthy sperm (the male reproductive cell).	
Seminal vesicles: Two small pouches found at base of bladder. Produce thick fluid that helps nourish and carry sperm.	
Testicles: Two egg-shaped glands that produce sperm.	
Epididymis: Tube at back of each testicle that joins urethra.	
Penis: Made of two parts: shaft (main part) and glans (tip, sometimes called head). Penis delivers sperm and urine through urethra. Made of spongy tissue. Sometimes the spongy tissue fills with blood and penis becomes hard (erection). Usually happens when male is sexually aroused, but can happen unexpectedly during puberty. (Wet dream: Where a boy gets an erection, and sperm – containing semen – is ejaculated, while sleeping.)	

Reproduction crossword

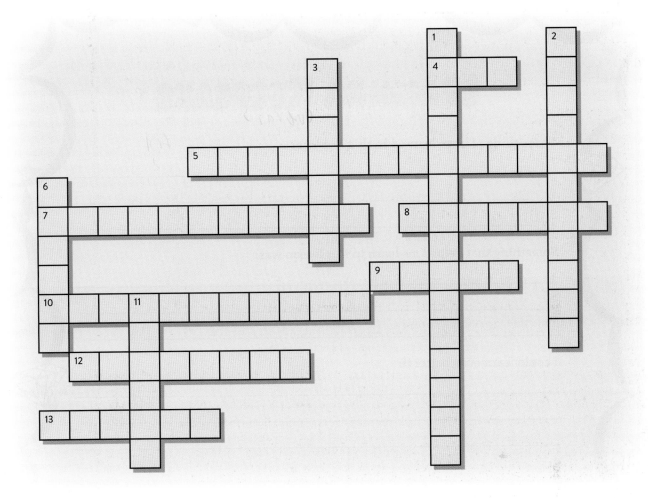

Across

4 The female reproductive cell.

5 Thin tubes that connect the ovaries to the uterus.

7 Another name for the lining of the womb.

8 A muscular bag that holds urine.

9 The male reproductive cell.

10 The release of sperm from the erect penis.

12 Sometimes removed from the tip of the male penis, but it does not affect its function.

13 Narrow muscular tube which connects the uterus to outside of the body.

Down

1 These produce a fluid which helps to carry sperm.

2 A thin tube carrying semen to the urethra.

3 External sac that holds and keeps the testicles at the proper temperature.

6 These produce sperm.

11 Neck of the womb through which the baby passes during childbirth.

LEARNING KEEPSAKE

Three things I have learned in this lesson are:

1. _____

2. _____

3. _____

Something that helped me learn in this lesson was:

_____

_____

_____

I could learn even better if:

_____

_____

_____

_____ has shared this Learning Keepsake with me _____

Name of student   *Parent's/Guardian's signature*

LESSON 26

Sexual Intercourse and Conception

Learning outcome: 3.6

responsible   aware

By the end of this lesson you will:

↝ understand human conception

KEYWORDS

Intercourse
Conception
Menstruation

The changes that take place during puberty are preparing you to potentially become a parent one day. In this lesson we will look at how conception occurs.

The reproduction story

When a man and a woman have sexual intercourse a baby may be conceived (made). This happens when the male sex cell (sperm) fuses with the female sex cell (egg). The meeting of the two cells is able to happen through a process called sexual intercourse.

INDIVIDUAL ACTIVITY

Gathering data

Complete the following cloze test using what you have learned and remember about the female and male reproductive systems from the previous lesson.

THE JOURNEY OF THE EGG/OVUM

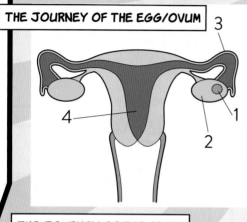

3
4
1
2

THE JOURNEY OF THE SPERM

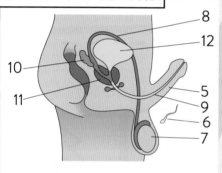

10
11
8
12
5
9
6
7

Each month in a woman's body, an 1. _egg_ ripens in one of her 2. _Ovarios_. In a process called ovulation, it is released and travels down the 3. _folopian tube_. In the days before ovulation, the 4. _Urures_ is preparing for the growth of the foetus by building up a thick, soft lining made of tissue and blood.

penis	urethra	testicles
uterus	prostate gland	seminal vesicles
vas deferens	bladder	egg/ovum
ovaries	Fallopian tube	sperm

When a man and woman express their love for each other by having sex, their bodies react in different ways. The man's 5. _Penis_ fills with blood and becomes hard. This is called an erection. The woman's vagina becomes moist. This makes it possible for sexual intercourse to take place. When the penis enters the vagina, 6. _____ produced in the 7. _____ are released and travel up along the long thin tube called the 8. _vas deferens_ all the way to the 9. _Urunil_. Along the way sperm mixes with fluids from the 10. _____ _____ and 11. _____ _____. This fluid, called semen, helps the sperm to swim. When the penis is ready to release semen, a valve blocks off the 12. _____, so urine cannot escape. Millions of sperm leave the penis and enter the vagina in a process called ejaculation. These sperm swim from the vagina through the cervix towards the Fallopian tube.

Fertilisation

If one of the sperm penetrates the egg in the Fallopian tube and the nuclei of the sperm and egg fuse, fertilisation occurs. The fertilised egg forms a cell that begins to divide and subdivide. It then travels to the uterus and continues to grow.

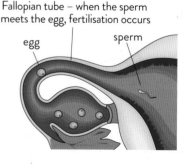

Fallopian tube – when the sperm meets the egg, fertilisation occurs

egg

sperm

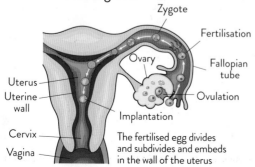

Zygote
Fertilisation
Ovary
Fallopian tube
Ovulation
Uterus
Uterine wall
Implantation
Cervix
Vagina

The fertilised egg divides and subdivides and embeds in the wall of the uterus

Once in the womb, the fertilised egg divides into the embryo and the placenta and embeds itself in the lining of the uterus. This is called implantation. The placenta will nourish the growing baby.

The menstrual cycle

If the egg is not fertilised, it doesn't attach to the wall of the uterus. The brain sends a message to the uterus lining telling it that it isn't needed any more. When this happens, the uterus sheds the lining and it passes through the cervix into the vagina and out of the female body. This is a called menstruation or, more commonly, the female period. It lasts approximately 2 to 7 days. As soon as the period occurs, the process begins again. This whole process is called the menstrual cycle.

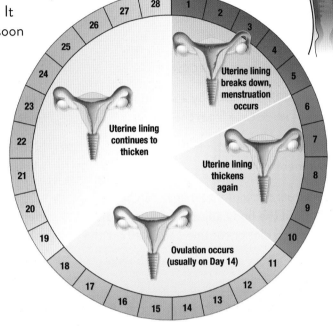

Menstrual fluid passing through cervix and vagina

If egg is not fertilised, the lining of the uterus breaks down

Uterine lining breaks down, menstruation occurs

Uterine lining thickens again

Uterine lining continues to thicken

Ovulation occurs (usually on Day 14)

AGE OF CONSENT

In Ireland, it is illegal to have sex with anyone under the age of 17.

INDIVIDUAL ACTIVITY

Evaluating data

Read the ten sentences that lay out the different steps to conception. Put them in the correct order by numbering them 1–10.

Sperm travels through the cervix and uterus and into the Fallopian tubes.	
The fertilised egg forms a cell that starts to divide and multiply.	
The man places his erect penis in the woman's vagina.	
If ovulation has occurred, one sperm cell meets one egg in the Fallopian tube and fertilisation (conception) occurs.	
A couple decide they would like to have a baby.	
The woman is now pregnant and the foetus will grow in her womb for the next nine months.	
Sperm cells leave the penis (ejaculation) and enter the vagina.	
Sperm cells leave the testicles and travel up the vas deferens.	
The fertilised egg travels down the Fallopian tube and into the uterus.	
Once in the uterus, the fertilised egg divides into the embryo and placenta and implants itself in the wall of the uterus.	

Some interesting facts

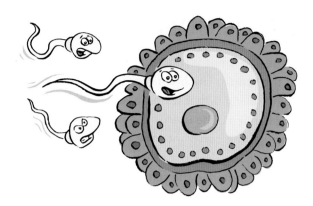

- Sperm can live for up to 5–7 days from the time of ejaculation.

- Only one sperm can penetrate an egg. As soon as the egg has been penetrated a barrier forms to prevent another sperm from entering.

- A female egg is about the size of a full stop.

- A woman is born with approximately one million immature eggs in her ovaries.

- An egg must be fertilised by a sperm within 48 hours of its release from the ovary.

- Eggs are pushed along the Fallopian tubes by the movement of tiny hairs.

- The menstrual cycle of a teenager can be irregular until the body adjusts. Stress, illness and changes in diet or routine can all affect the menstrual cycle.

- The first period is called the menarche.

- Approximately 200–500 million sperm can be released during each ejaculation.

- Non-identical twins (fraternal twins) happen when two eggs are released at the same time and are fertilised by two different sperm.

- Identical twins happen when one fertilised egg splits and develops two babies with exactly the same genetic information.

INDIVIDUAL ACTIVITY

Reflecting on my learning

On a piece of paper, write down one question or comment about what you have learned today. When you are finished, fold the paper and hand it to your teacher.

LEARNING KEEPSAKE

Three things I have learned in this lesson are:

1. _____
2. _____
3. _____

Something that helped me learn in this lesson was:

_____

_____

_____

I could learn even better if:

_____

_____

_____

_____ has shared this Learning Keepsake with me _____

Name of student   *Parent's/Guardian's signature*

LESSON 27
Gender Stereotypes and Discrimination

Learning outcomes: 1.4, 1.8, 3.9

responsible · connected · respected · aware

By the end of this lesson you will:
- ◆ have explored aspects of gender stereotyping
- ◆ understand how gender stereotyping can influence our attitudes and behaviours

KEYWORDS

Gender stereotype

Identity

Debating/
Discussing

CLASS ACTIVITY

Your teacher will read out the following words. For each word, put one hand up if you think it's a 'girl thing', put both hands up if you think it's a 'boy thing', or keep your hands down if you think it could be a 'both' thing.

- dolls
- carer
- dancing
- flowers
- drummer
- pink
- surgeon
- nurse

- cars
- muscles
- diet drinks
- scientist
- blue
- apron
- beautician

- engineer
- work overalls
- glitter
- mathematician
- plumber
- strong
- pilot

Was there agreement in the class regarding what were considered 'girl things' or 'boy things'? Why do you think you answered the way you did?

Gender stereotyping

Gender norms and stereotyping are ingrained in us from a very young age. Baby girls are often dressed in pink, and baby boys in blue. Toys are gifted based on gender, the pretty baby doll for the girl and the toolbox for the boy. This stereotyping continues throughout childhood into adolescence and then adulthood. As adults, we can be influenced and limited by these stereotypes.

Gender stereotyping means having certain expectations of people because they happen to be male or female. These expectations can limit who we can be and what we can do and the choices we think we can make, as males and females.

Listening and expressing myself

In pairs, write some common male and female stereotypes in and around each figure.

INDIVIDUAL ACTIVITY

Reflecting

Now, based on what you and your partner wrote, answer these questions:

1. Where do you think these stereotypes come from?

   _____

   _____

2. How do they influence how males and females act and behave in their daily lives?

   _____

   _____

3. How does it influence how males and females treat each other?

   _____

   _____

4. If a female doesn't fit into a certain stereotype and acts differently, how might this affect her?

   _____

   _____

5. If a male doesn't fit into a certain stereotype and acts differently, how might this affect him?

   _____

   _____

6. Do stereotypes influence the choices we make about what career we might like to have?

   _____

   _____

7. In what way does gender stereotyping limit us in terms of behaviour, appearance, interests, etc.?

   _____

   _____

Gender stereotypes are so fixed in our minds that sometimes we don't question them. Our culture bombards us with messages about what it means to be male and female. We need to take a step back and see how these messages affect us and in many cases how they affect our behaviour and our choices. The most important thing to remember is that we should not allow gender stereotypes to limit us in what we want to do with and in our lives, whether we are male or female.

INDIVIDUAL ACTIVITY

Learning creatively

Although there have been huge changes in society over the years, gender stereotypes still exist. These stereotypes are not healthy and fail to recognise that every person is unique. It is important to respect each person's individuality.

Using the heading 'Break the Mould', design a poster to combat gender stereotyping in society. Some examples of posters are given as inspiration.

Gender Roles in Society

Break the mould

He Can Do It!

Break the mould

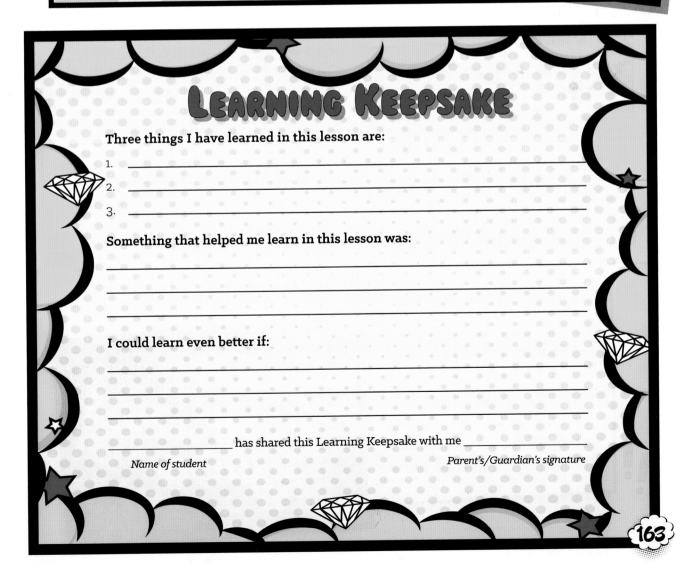

LEARNING KEEPSAKE

Three things I have learned in this lesson are:

1. _____

2. _____

3. _____

Something that helped me learn in this lesson was:

_____

_____

_____

I could learn even better if:

_____

_____

_____

_____ has shared this Learning Keepsake with me _____

Name of student   *Parent's/Guardian's signature*

163

LESSON 28
Sexuality, Sexual Identity and Sexual Orientation

Learning outcomes: 1.4, 3.9

 responsible connected respected aware

By the end of this lesson you will:

→ have learned about the issues faced by gay, lesbian, bisexual and transgender people

→ know why it is important to respect and accept all people, whatever their sexual orientation

KEYWORDS

Lesbian	Homophobic
Gay	Coming out
Bisexual	Diversity

USEFUL WEBSITES

www.lgbt.ie A support and education organisation that works to help and enhance the lives of LGBTQ+ people in Ireland. **Phone 1890 929 539**.

www.belongto.org Offers support and advice for lesbian, gay, bisexual and transgender young people.

www.teni.ie Transgender Equality Network Ireland (TENI) provides information and support to transgender people and their families.

Sometimes we might be a little unsure as to what different words related to sexuality and gender mean, e.g. 'sexual orientation', 'gender identity'. The following activity will help you to understand the meaning of different terms.

PAIR ACTIVITY

In pairs, read each definition and match it to the correct word or words by writing the number of the definition in the box beside its name.

Homophobia		Sexuality		Gender identity		Transgender	
Heterosexism		Bisexual		Diversity acceptance		Ally	
Transition		Sexual orientation		Coming out		Heterosexual	
LGBTQ+		Homosexual					

1. Someone who is attracted romantically, physically and/or emotionally to both sexes.

2. Someone whose gender differs from the one they were given when they were born. They may identify as male or female, or they may feel that neither label fits them.

3. Describes a person's romantic, emotional or sexual attraction to another person. It is associated with a person's feelings and identity.

4. A person who is attracted to someone of the opposite sex.

5. The assumption that everyone is heterosexual or that opposite-sex attractions and relationships are both the norm and superior.

6. A person who is attracted romantically, emotionally and sexually to someone of the same sex.

7. Negative feelings, attitudes or believes directed at non-heterosexual people. A person can be a victim just because other people think they are gay, lesbian or bisexual, even if they are not.

8. Accepting and respecting the variety of different people in a community.

9. People who do not identify as LGBTQ+ but support this community by standing against bullying and harassment.

10. The process a transgender person may go through to move from one gender to another.

11. A person's internal feeling of being male or female or transgender, regardless of the sex listed on their birth certificate.

12. Stands for 'lesbian, gay, bisexual, transgender and queer'. The '+' symbol includes those who may be questioning their sexuality, identify as asexual (not attracted to either gender in any romantic or sexual way) or who are 'intersex' (general term for a variety of physical conditions where a person is born with a reproductive or sexual anatomy that doesn't seem to fit the typical definitions of female or male).

13. The term used to describe the process a person goes through in which they understand and accept that they are lesbian, gay, bisexual or transgender and develop the confidence to tell other people.

14. Part of being human. Not just about sexual activity, but what it means to be male or female and how we express that in what wear, how we behave, who we are attracted to, how we feel about ourselves and others.

Being LGBTQ+ in Ireland today

Thankfully, today's society is a more open place than it was in the past, and more LGBTQ+ people feel comfortable 'coming out'. This is largely due to the fact that they feel they have support from their family and friends, school, community and neighbourhood.

Despite this, life can still be difficult for some LGBTQ+ people as they feel they do not get support from others. They fear a bad reaction if they come out. Lesbian, gay, bisexual and transgender students are part of every student body, yet some LGBTQ+ students still report having negative experiences in school. A national study of the mental health and wellbeing of LGBTQ+ teenagers in Ireland in 2016 found that:

67% had witnessed bullying of LGBTQ+ students in their school
48% had personally experienced LGBTQ+ bullying by fellow students
Only 25% rated their school's LGBTQ+ friendliness as '7 out of 10' or higher
Just 1 in 5 felt they completely belonged in their school as an LGBTQ+ student
Only 44% said they were positively affirmed about their LGBTQ+ identity
1 in 4 missed or skipped school or school events to avoid negative treatment due to being LGBTQ+
1 in 4 considered leaving school early (before final state examinations) because of negative treatment they had received as an LGBTQ+ student
5% did leave early

We all have a sexual identity. It is a natural part of who we are, and we should not be ashamed of it. It is important to respect other people's sexual orientation and gender identity. Bullying or judging someone because of their sexual orientation is wrong. We should not tolerate homophobic or transphobic bullying. We should treat everyone with the dignity and respect they deserve.

Did you realise?

- 5–10% of our population identify as lesbian, gay or bisexual.
- The average age for a person to become aware of their sexual identity is 12.
- The average age for coming out is 16.
- The legal age for having sex in Ireland is 17. It is the same for people of all sexual orientations.
- The age of realisation of trans identity is generally much younger than sexual orientation identity.
- Sexual orientation is not a choice and cannot be changed.
- You cannot tell if someone is straight, lesbian, gay, bisexual or transgender by looking at them.
- The Equality Status Act prohibits the harassment of individuals based on their sexual orientation.
- Same-sex marriage has been legal in Ireland since 2015.
- There are support groups for people struggling with their sexuality.

Respecting difference/
Making the world a better place

In pairs, write down five things your school could do to ensure that **LGBTQ+** students feel respected and have a positive experience while at school (e.g. in SPHE class, the student council, anti-bullying policy, code of behaviour). Then write down five things you could do (or not do) as individuals to ensure an **LGBTQ+** person feels safe and welcome in your company.

Supportive school environment	Supportive individual behaviour
1.	1.
2.	2.
3.	3.
4.	4.
5.	5.

Co-operating/
Respecting difference

As a group, design and run a poster campaign that would help to support young LGBTQ+ students in your school. Come up with a slogan to accompany your poster campaign and include images of inclusivity and acceptance. Here are two examples to inspire you.

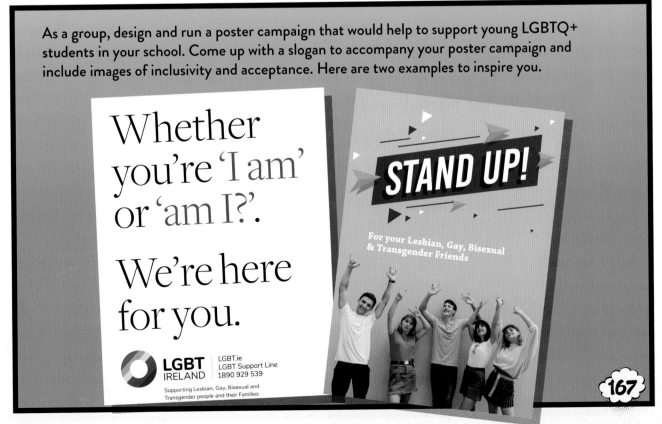

HELP AND SUPPORT

The National LGBT Helpline provides a confidential listening, support and information service to lesbian, gay, bisexual and transgender people. The service is also used by people who are questioning if they might be LGBTQ+, as well as the family and friends of LGBTQ+ people and professionals looking for information. The service is volunteer-run and operates Monday to Friday from 7 p.m. to 9 p.m, Saturday and Sunday 3 p.m. to 6 p.m.

Website: www.lgbt.ie

Call: 1890 929 539

BeLonGTo Youth Service is the national youth service for lesbian, gay, bisexual and transgender young people aged between 14 and 23. There are youth services located in most areas around the country.

Website: www.belongto.org

Email: info@belongto.ie

Transgender Equality Network Ireland (TENI) provides information and support to transgender people and their families.

Website: www.teni.ie

Email: office@teni.ie

LEARNING KEEPSAKE

Three things I have learned in this lesson are:

1. _____

2. _____

3. _____

Something that helped me learn in this lesson was:

_____

_____

_____

I could learn even better if:

_____

_____

_____

_____ has shared this Learning Keepsake with me _____

Name of student   *Parent's/Guardian's signature*

MEET THE CHALLENGE

Strand 3 Topic 3
A REPORT ON GENDERED ADVERTISING

Learning outcomes: 3.9, 3.10, 3.11

Working in groups of three or four, choose three advertisements that are aimed at young people to see if they use gender stereotypes to sell their products or services. You can choose advertisements you see on television, in magazines or on social media sites (or a mixture of all of these). Aim to review a mix of advertisements: those aimed at teenage boys, those aimed at teenage girls, and those aimed at both boys and girls. Write a report on your findings, including the following elements:

○ a title indicating what your report is about

○ a clear structure: an introduction stating what your study is about, the types of advertisements you are examining, and where and when you saw them

○ a short paragraph reporting your findings, e.g. the roles given to the people in the advertisements, or the customers suggested by the marketing

○ a short paragraph reviewing these findings: whether the adverts conform to and reinforce gender stereotypes or whether they are more 'gender neutral' (aimed equally at both boys and girls despite the product)

○ a paragraph stating any recommendations or advice for marketing companies to help them avoid reinforcing gender stereotypes

MENTAL HEALTH & WELLBEING

STRAND 4

LESSON 29
Recognising and Expressing Feelings

Learning outcome: 4.1

responsible   connected   resilient   aware

By the end of this lesson you will:

↠ be aware of the importance of recognising your feelings

↠ be aware of appropriate ways in which to express your feelings

KEYWORDS

Appropriate

Inappropriate

Emotions

Feelings

USEFUL WEBSITE

www.barnardos.ie/teenhelp Search the 'Finding Help' section for contact details of organisations, websites and helplines that provide information, advice and support for teenagers.

Feelings are our bodies' way of telling us what is going on inside us, so it is very important to pay attention to them. Once you have identified your feelings, you can manage them and learn to express them more appropriately. Strong feelings like anger and fear can sometimes overwhelm us, so once we learn to recognise and regulate these feelings we can become more in control of situations, instead of these feelings controlling us.

INDIVIDUAL ACTIVITY

Knowing myself

Below are examples of common feelings. Pick five from the list and complete the sentences.

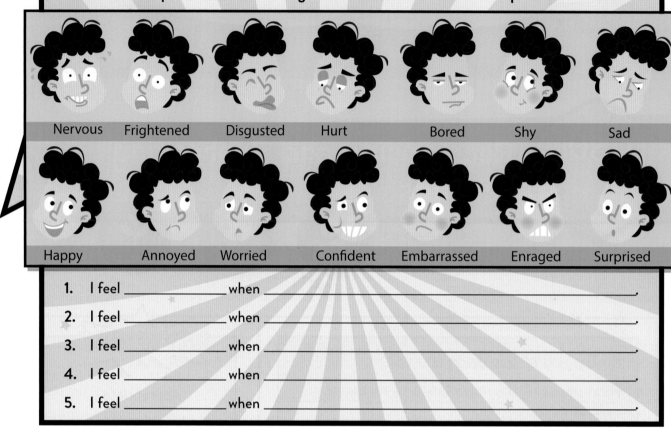

Nervous	Frightened	Disgusted	Hurt	Bored	Shy	Sad

Happy	Annoyed	Worried	Confident	Embarrassed	Enraged	Surprised

1. I feel _____ when _____.
2. I feel _____ when _____.
3. I feel _____ when _____.
4. I feel _____ when _____.
5. I feel _____ when _____.

Understanding body clues

Our bodies can give us the best clues as to how we are feeling. For example, if you are nervous you might get butterflies in your stomach, your muscles might tense up or your heart might start racing. Have you ever heard of the term 'gut feeling'? This is another example of a body clue. It is the feeling you get inside if you feel something is right or wrong.

INDIVIDUAL ACTIVITY

Thinking creatively and critically

Look at the different feelings below and write in the different body clues a person may get if they were experiencing this feeling.

B. Sad _____
_____

A. Happy _____
_____

D. Scared _____

_____

_____

C. Angry _____

_____

_____

E. Anxious _____

_____

_____

Managing our feelings

It is important to be able to recognise our feelings in order to manage them effectively. Paying attention to body clues can play a big part in this. If we can catch our feelings early when they are small and easy to manage, we can prevent them from getting worse. For example, if we start to feel angry in a situation, we can take ourselves away from the situation or count to ten in our heads. This can give us time to calm down. Or if we are beginning to feel stressed, we can practise deep breathing exercises.

Our body thermometer

How we feel will vary in intensity from situation to situation, and the way we respond differs from person to person. Our bodies are a good indicator of the level of intensity of our feelings. We can think of our bodies as our feelings thermometer.

If you had an exam coming up, you might be a little nervous, so you might rate this feeling as 1 or 2 on the scale in terms of intensity. However, having to make a presentation in front of your classmates could make you extremely nervous, and so you might rate this as level 4 or 5 on the thermometer. For feelings such as anger, fear or worry, the trick is to be able to 'catch' or recognise your feelings early, before they escalate to levels 4 or 5 on the thermometer, and then you will be in a better position to cope with and manage them.

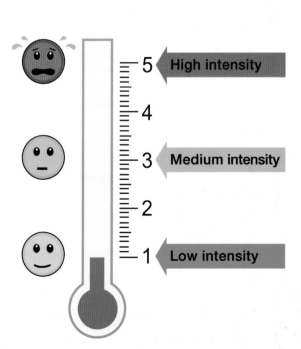

INDIVIDUAL ACTIVITY

Knowing myself

Look back on the first activity you did in this lesson ('I felt ... when ...'). In the boxes above each thermometer, rewrite these statements. On the matching thermometer, colour in the thermometer to show the intensity of your feeling. Remember, 1 is low intensity and 5 is high intensity. The higher up you go, the stronger the feeling.

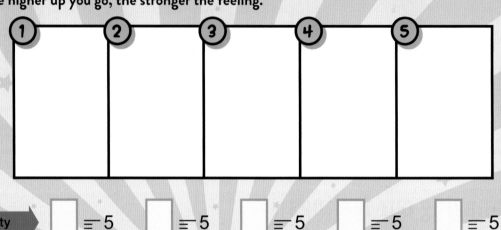

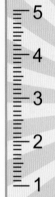

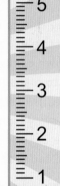

High intensity

Medium intensity

Low intensity

CLASS ACTIVITY

Debating/
Discussing

If we learn to recognise our feelings, we can manage them better. Recognising our feelings can also help us to respond better in difficult situations. When we act in the moment, when the intensity of our emotions is high, we can say or do things we don't mean. Read the following story and then consider the responses, explaining why they may be appropriate or inappropriate.

Feeling hurt

Jane is a First Year student. Since she started secondary school she has been very friendly with Ruth. One day, just before basketball training, Jane overhears Ruth talking about her behind her back with two other students, Sarah and Lorna.

Inappropriate responses	Appropriate responses
Jane rushes up to Ruth and shouts at her.	Jane tells Ruth she overheard her and that she is hurt.
Jane ignores Ruth for two months.	Jane decides to forget about it because Ruth has been a good friend up to now.
Jane pretends she didn't hear anything but promises herself that she will get back at Ruth.	Jane makes a joke of it with Ruth, letting Ruth know that she has heard the conversation but that she forgives her.
Why are these responses inappropriate?	*Why are these responses appropriate?*

INDIVIDUAL ACTIVITY

Knowing myself

Read the following two scenarios and write down appropriate and inappropriate responses to each.

Scenario 1

You are training with the school football team. The coach has made it very clear that commitment is really valued, and he has told the team at the start of the season that he will only play people who attend training. One of the other players, who is very talented, has missed a lot of training sessions. Just before the first championship match you learn that you have been dropped and the other player has been picked ahead of you.

1. How would you feel in this scenario?

   _____

2. What would be an inappropriate response to the situation?

   _____

3. Why would this be inappropriate?

   _____

4. What would be an appropriate response to the situation?

   _____

5. Why would this be appropriate?

   _____

Scenario 2

Your teacher has set your group a project to complete for class. One of the group members is very bossy and keeps forcing his opinions on your group. You really want to have some input but you are finding it difficult to make yourself heard.

1. How would you feel in this scenario?

   _____

2. What would be an inappropriate response to the situation?

   _____

3. Why would this be inappropriate?

   _____

4. What would be an appropriate response to the situation?

   _____

5. Why would this be appropriate?

   _____

Listening/
expressing myself

CLASS ACTIVITY

Now compare and discuss your answers to these two scenarios as a class.

INDIVIDUAL ACTIVITY

Knowing myself

Feelings are never right or wrong – they just are. However, people can control how they express their feelings. It is important to respect other people's feelings when expressing your own.

1. Write down a time when you expressed your feelings in an inappropriate way.

_____

_____

2. Suggest a more appropriate way you could have expressed how you felt in this situation.

_____

_____

LEARNING KEEPSAKE

Three things I have learned in this lesson are:

1. _____
2. _____
3. _____

Something that helped me learn in this lesson was:

_____

_____

_____

I could learn even better if:

_____

_____

_____

_____ has shared this Learning Keepsake with me _____

Name of student *Parent's/Guardian's signature*

LESSON 30
Respecting My Feelings and the Feelings of Others

Learning outcome: 4.2

responsible

connected

aware

respected

By the end of this lesson you will:

•→ be more aware of other people's feelings

•→ understand the importance of empathy

KEYWORDS

Facial expressions

Gestures

Postures

Empathy

Recognising and expressing our feelings is very important because it helps us to acknowledge, recognise and respect the feelings of others. When we can understand how other people are feeling and thinking, we are better able to support them. This is called empathy.

EMPATHY: the ability to understand how another person is feeling. It means trying to put yourself in their shoes, and thinking about how you would feel in the situation and how you would like others to help you if you were in a similar situation.

INDIVIDUAL ACTIVITY

Thinking creatively and critically

1. Look at the images below and write down how you think the person in each image is feeling.
   Explain why you think this, making reference to their posture, facial expression, gestures, etc.
   Write down what you might say in each situation, and what you might feel if you were in their
   shoes.

1. How do you think this person is feeling?
   _____

2. Why do you think this?
   _____
   _____
   _____

3. What might you say to a person in this
   situation?
   _____
   _____
   _____

4. How might you feel if you were in their
   shoes?
   _____
   _____
   _____

1. How do you think this person is feeling?
   _____

2. Why do you think this?
   _____
   _____
   _____

3. What might you say to a person in this
   situation?
   _____
   _____
   _____

4. How might you feel if you were in their
   shoes?
   _____
   _____
   _____

1. How do you think this person is feeling?
   _____

2. Why do you think this?
   _____
   _____

3. What might you say to a person in this situation?
   _____
   _____

4. How might you feel if you were in their shoes?
   _____
   _____

1. How do you think this person is feeling?

   _____

2. Why do you think this?

   _____

   _____

   _____

3. What might you say to a person in this situation?

   _____

   _____

   _____

4. How might you feel if you were in their shoes?

   _____

   _____

   _____

1. How do you think this person is feeling?

   _____

2. Why do you think this?

   _____

   _____

   _____

3. What might you say to a person in this situation?

   _____

   _____

   _____

4. How might you feel if you were in their shoes?

   _____

   _____

   _____

2. **Now delve a little deeper into what you think regarding expressing emotions, if and how men and women express emotions differently, and if/why it is important to be empathetic towards others by answering the following questions:**

(a) List three emotions that are considered acceptable:

   (i) _____

   (ii) _____

   (iii) _____

(b) List three emotions that are considered unacceptable:

   (i) _____

   (ii) _____

   (iii) _____

(c) Why do you think some emotions are more acceptable than others?

   _____

   _____

(d) Do men and women express their emotions differently? If yes, how?

   _____

   _____

(e) Why is it important to be able to recognise other people's feelings?

   _____

   _____

Thinking creatively
and critically

As a group, read the situations below. Imagine you know the person in each situation. Discuss how they might be feeling and answer the questions.

A

Mark thinks he is gay.

How do you think he is feeling?

_____

_____

_____

What thoughts might he have?

_____

_____

_____

How might he be behaving?

_____

_____

_____

How could you or others support him?

_____

_____

_____

_____

B

Lara's parents are constantly arguing.

How do you think she is feeling?

_____

_____

_____

What thoughts might she have?

_____

_____

_____

How might she be behaving?

_____

_____

_____

How could you or others support her?

_____

_____

_____

_____

C

Greg's dog died.

How do you think he is feeling?

_____

_____

_____

What thoughts might he have?

_____

_____

_____

How might he be behaving?

_____

_____

_____

How could you or others support him?

_____

_____

_____

_____

D

Joanne has to move to a new foster home even though she is happy in the one she is in now.

How do you think she is feeling?

_____

_____

_____

What thoughts might she have?

_____

_____

_____

How might she be behaving?

_____

_____

_____

How could you or others support her?

_____

_____

_____

E

Jonah is being bullied by other students.

How do you think he is feeling?

_____

_____

_____

What thoughts might he have?

_____

_____

How might he be behaving?

_____

_____

How could you or others support him?

_____

_____

_____

F

Vivienne shared some private information with her friend, Rob, and he has since shared it with others. Rob even posted publicly online about the secret.

How do you think she is feeling?

_____

_____

What thoughts might she have?

_____

_____

How might she be behaving?

_____

_____

How could you or others support her?

_____

_____

Thinking creatively and critically

In pairs, think about two challenges people in your school face and about how you could support them.

Challenge 1	Challenge 2
What is the challenge?	What is the challenge?
How could you support them?	How could you support them?

Thinking creatively
and critically

Writing

INDIVIDUAL ACTIVITY

Using what you have learned in today's lesson, complete this activity. Walk in someone else's shoes by writing what you can do/say/behave should you come across someone feeling in the ways listed.

Take a Walk in My Shoes!!

1. When someone is angry I can ...
2. When someone is embarrassed I can ...
3. When someone is anxious I can ...
4. When someone is disappointed I can ...
5 When someone is confused I can ...
6. When someone is frustrated I can ...
7. When someone is hurt I can ...
8. When someone is scared I can ...
9. When someone is sick I can ...
10. When someone is sad I can ...
11. When someone is proud I can ...
12. When someone is triumphant I can ...

LEARNING KEEPSAKE

Three things I have learned in this lesson are:

1. _____

2. _____

3. _____

Something that helped me learn in this lesson was:

_____

_____

_____

I could learn even better if:

_____

_____

_____

_____ has shared this Learning Keepsake with me _____

Name of student   *Parent's/Guardian's signature*

LESSON 31

Looking After My Mental Health and Wellbeing

Learning outcomes: 4.1, 4.3, 4.4, 4.5, 4.9

 responsible

 connected

 resilient

 respected

 aware

By the end of this lesson you will:

↠ be able to explain what it means to have positive mental health and wellbeing

↠ have developed skills to help you deal with the ups and downs of everyday life

KEYWORDS

Positive mental health

Poor mental health

USEFUL WEBSITES

www.**barnardos.ie** Provides tips and advice for young people on how to look after their wellbeing.

www.**kidshealth.org** Provides a range of information on issues affecting teenagers.

Feeling positive about ourselves and the world around us

Recognising our strengths and being resilient

Having healthy relationships with family and friends

Our mental health is an essential part of our overall wellbeing. For all people, be they young or old, having positive mental health means:

Being able to cope with stressful situations

Being able to deal with feelings and express them in a positive way

Being able to recognise difficult or sad situations and deal with them as they occur

Being able to empathise with others

 185

Just as we have physical health, we all have mental health. Our mental health operates along a scale from feeling well to feeling unwell. As a teenager, you will experience many new feelings and thoughts. There are times when you will feel up and there are times when you will feel down. You have a lot more responsibilities and demands now than when you were a child and you are still developing the skills and knowledge to cope with these added pressures. The important thing is to be able to manage life's demands so that you can maintain positive mental health.

INDIVIDUAL ACTIVITY

Knowing myself

Thinking about mental health, what can make us feel down and what can help us, answer these questions:

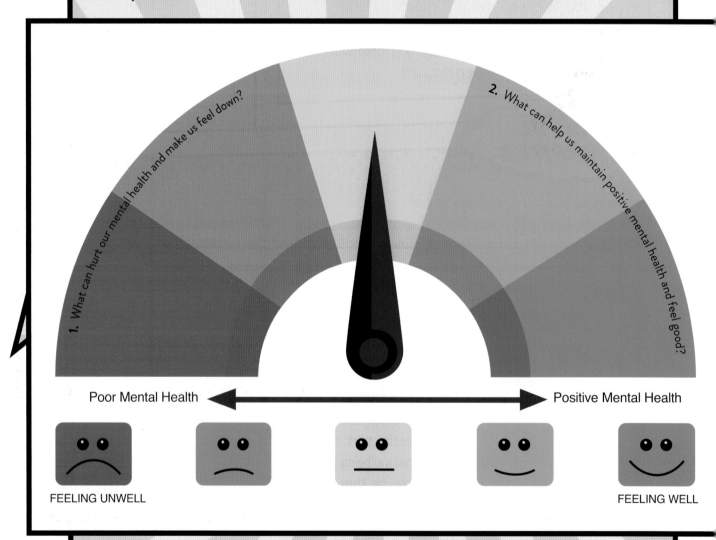

1. What can hurt our mental health and make us feel down?

2. What can help us maintain positive mental health and feel good?

Poor Mental Health ←→ Positive Mental Health

FEELING UNWELL   FEELING WELL

3. If we are feeling down or low, list all the actions and people that can help us to feel better.

_____

_____

_____

Managing our mental wellbeing

In earlier lessons we looked at how to look after our physical wellbeing. We saw that it is important to eat well, exercise and look after ourselves physically. It is important to realise that we can also take care of and manage our own mental wellbeing. Here are five simple actions you can do in everyday life to improve your mental wellbeing.

Five ways to wellbeing

Connect

Make time each day to connect with people around you at home, in school and in your local community. This can include interacting with your family members and arranging to meet friends. Reducing your screen time when in company can also help you connect with others.

Be active

Evidence shows that there is a link between being physically active and good mental wellbeing. Find activities you enjoy and can fit into your life. Take some time to exercise, go for a walk somewhere you like, cycle with a friend, dance. You may not like exercising, but try something you might enjoy.

Take notice

Take time to stop and become aware of the world around you. Paying attention to our thoughts and feelings can improve our mental health. Stay in the moment whether you are walking, eating or talking. Being in the moment is also called mindfulness.

MINDFULNESS BREATHING EXERCISE

Try to undertake this breathing exercise every day, building up to ten minutes.

- Sit on your chair with your back straight.
- Place your hands on your lap with the palms facing upwards.
- Place your feet firmly on the ground.
- Close your eyes or keep them focused on a fixed spot.
- Pay close attention to your breath, noticing your in-breath and your out-breath.
- You will find that your mind wanders. This is fine, just bring your attention back to your breath.

Keep learning

Always push yourself to try new things. Take on new responsibilities. Push yourself outside your comfort zone. Learn a new skill, start baking, take up a new hobby, volunteer with an organisation – it doesn't matter what it is, and it doesn't matter how big or small an activity it is. The important thing is to keep trying new things and to not limit yourself or your world.

Help or support others

Helping and supporting others, or doing small, kind things for them, or even just thanking others and being grateful for what they might do for you can be very good for our mental wellbeing. Doing good things for the environment will also have a positive effect on our mental health. So thank someone, or give someone a (sincere) compliment, or do something helpful for someone, even without letting them know it was you who did it. Pick up rubbish and be mindful of your surroundings. Doing these random acts of kindness will not only make others feel better, they'll make you feel better too.

 INDIVIDUAL ACTIVITY

Thinking creatively and critically

Now consider each of these areas in relation to your own mental wellbeing. What are you already doing or what will you do to manage your own mental wellbeing?

1. CONNECT

5. HELP OR SUPPORT OTHERS

2. BE ACTIVE

MY MENTAL WELLBEING

4. KEEP LEARNING

3. TAKE NOTICE

LEARNING KEEPSAKE

Three things I have learned in this lesson are:

1. _____

2. _____

3. _____

Something that helped me learn in this lesson was:

_____

_____

_____

I could learn even better if:

_____

_____

_____

_____ has shared this Learning Keepsake with me _____

Name of student   *Parent's/Guardian's signature*

MEET THE CHALLENGE
Strand 4 Topic 1
MY WELLBEING ACTIVITIES

Learning outcomes: 4.1, 4.2, 4.3, 4.8

See how many of the following activities you can undertake over the next week or couple of weeks. They will help you improve your wellbeing.

◯ Tick them off as you complete them.

◯ If you think of any more that you can do, write them in the spaces at the bottom.

Remember: taking care of our mental health is something we have to work at. You won't be able to do all these things at once, or you might find that your enthusiasm wanes, but the important thing is to keep trying. Slowly but surely, you will find that some of them become second nature to you. All of this will benefit your mental health and, therefore, you.

Monday	Tuesday	Wednesday	Thursday	Friday	Saturday	Sunday
Eat lunch with someone new.	Try to complete a crossword or word search.	Sort out your notes for school.	Do an act of kindness for someone you know.	Compliment someone you interact with.	Get rid of five things you never use.	Try something new.
Put your phone away for a few hours and talk to family members.	Call to a friend or family member.	Make a conscious decision to smile five times today.	Hold the door for someone.	Listen to your happy song.	Tell someone important how much they mean to you.	Eat healthily today.
Do ten minutes of a relaxation technique.	Clean out a wardrobe and organise your clothes.	Go for a walk without your phone.	Prepare a healthy lunch for tomorrow.	Write down four things you are grateful for.	Sit down and focus on your breathing for five minutes.	Be sure to thank everyone who does something for you/ gives you something today.

Drink eight glasses of water.	Write down three things you are happy about.	Start reading a new book.	Write down three positive statements you could say to yourself.	Take a picture of something that makes you happy.	Do something that makes you happy.	Continue reading a new book or watch a movie.
Stay off Instagram for the day.	Send a nice text message to someone.	Do some mindful breathing.	Before going to bed, put away your clothes and tidy up your room.	Take time to check in with someone.	Do some activity that you enjoy.	Write down three things you like about yourself.

TOPIC 2
Dealing with Tough Times

LESSON 32 — Positive Self-Talk

Learning outcomes: 4.2, 4.8, 4.9

 responsible
 connected
 resilient
 aware

By the end of this lesson you will:

◆ have explored how your thinking habits impact on your ability to read situations and cope during challenging times

KEYWORDS

Optimist

Pessimist

What is self-talk?

Most of us may not even realise it, but as we are going about our day we are constantly talking to ourselves in our heads. This type of talk is called self-talk. We all engage in self-talk, we can't help it. When we're in challenging situations, helpful self-talk makes us feel good or better about ourselves, for example, 'I'm doing the best I can', 'This isn't so bad', 'I can do this if I put in the effort'. Here we are being resilient. However, some of our self-talk can be unhelpful, unrealistic and only serves to put us down, for example, 'Everyone is better than me', 'Nothing ever goes right for me', 'Typical, I couldn't do it'. We wouldn't talk that way to our best friend, so why would we talk that way to ourselves?

It is important to be aware of our self-talk and how it affects how we feel and how we act. It's also important to know that negative thoughts are just that – thoughts. Just because you're thinking them, that doesn't make them true. When you have negative thoughts (thoughts that aren't going to be helpful to you in any way), try to recognise that the thought is unhelpful to you, and then let the thought go. Easier said than done, but this is something that needs to be practised.

An **optimist** looks on the bright side of situations. They will use helpful self-talk to deal with a situation, making them calmer, more hopeful and better able to cope with challenges. They see the glass as being half full.

A **pessimist** will focus on the worst-case scenario. They use negative self-talk to deal with a situation, making them frustrated, hopeless and less likely to overcome challenges. They see the glass as being half empty.

GROUP ACTIVITY

Learning with others

Reading with understanding

As a group, read the following scenarios, and then in the relevant columns below, fill in what you think the optimist and the pessimist would say in each scenario. In the remaining rows, add in three more scenarios where young people may use self-talk. The first one has been done for you.

SCENARIO	WHAT SELF-TALK WOULD THE OPTIMIST USE?	WHAT SELF-TALK WOULD THE PESSIMIST USE?
1. You have to do a group presentation for English class. You did one last week in Business Studies but you were extremely nervous: your hands were shaking and your voice was cracking.	'Even though I was nervous for Business Studies I still got through it. Most people get nervous in these situations, so I am no different.'	'I felt really embarrassed the last time and everyone probably thought I was stupid because my hands were shaking so much. I don't think I can go through it all again.'
2. You are playing in a game and you hear your manager calling you to come off.		
3. A person in your class has unfriended you on Facebook.		
4. You put a selfie on Instagram, and someone writes a nasty message about it.		

5. You have a cup match on Saturday. You played that team before and your team lost.		
6. You forgot you have an exam today in Geography class and you haven't studied for it.		
7. Your friend takes you aside quietly and tells you that you have body odour.		
8. You wear a new outfit today that you think is really nice, but when you meet your friends they laugh at you.		
9. You played a match and though you played really well, but when you came off the field your coach told you that you played terribly.		
10. Your best friend from primary school is in a different class and has made new friends. He doesn't seem to spend much time with you any more.		
11. One of your classmates is having a party on Friday night for their birthday. Everyone in the class seems to be invited except you.		
12.		
13.		
14.		

Unhelpful thinking habits

Here are some different types of unhelpful thinking habits.

Catastrophising: Imagining and believing that the worst thing will happen

Mountains and molehills: Where you exaggerate the facts; a small problem becomes a huge one; thinking something is the end of the world, e.g. 'I never have any luck' – in other words, making mountains out of molehills

Jumping to conclusions: Thinking you know what's going to happen in the future; sometimes called 'fortune-telling'

Mind-reading: Guessing what the other person is thinking and then believing that this must be the truth, e.g. you think someone is ignoring you because they didn't salute you but perhaps they didn't see you, or they were distracted

Black and white thinking: Believing someone or something can only be good or bad, right or wrong, with no in between

Compare and despair: Comparing ourselves to others and feeling we will never be as good as them/ as talented as them/as smart as them/as good-looking as them, etc.

Overgeneralising: Thinking because something happened once, it will happen again, e.g. you vow never to get in a lift again because you got stuck in one once

Shoulds and musts: Using statements like 'I should ...' or 'I must ...' to put pressure on yourself, or because you have unrealistic expectations of yourself, e.g. 'I should have won that game tonight – I'm rubbish. I must win the game next week, or I might as well give up.'

Self-criticism: Putting ourselves down or blaming ourselves for events even though we might not be totally responsible for them

Emotional reasoning: Assuming that because we feel a certain way, then it must be true

Changing our unhelpful self-talk takes time and practice, but the more we practise, the better we become at noticing it and changing it, or at least acknowledging it and allowing it to slip by. The more time we spend replacing unhelpful self-talk with more helpful self-talk, the more likely we are to feel in control of different things that are going on in our lives. Remember that everyone experiences negative self-talk, and everyone – absolutely everyone – experiences difficult scenarios in their lives, often every day! We all face these challenges, so it is important that we learn how to deal with them.

Tips for tackling unhelpful self-talk

☞ **Listen to your self-talk.** Is your self-talk helpful or unhelpful? Be aware of unhelpful thinking habits that you may have.

☞ **Challenge your self-talk.** Ask yourself questions like:

- ○ Is there actual evidence for what I'm thinking?
- ○ Am I only noticing the bad things?
- ○ Have I got my facts right?
- ○ How likely is this to happen?
- ○ Am I totally to blame for this?
- ○ How would someone else in my position see this?
- ○ Am I exaggerating the bad stuff?
- ○ What would I say to a friend in a similar situation?

☞ **Change your self-talk.** Make a list of all the positive things about yourself. Instead of saying things like 'I'll never be able to do this', try saying 'Is there anything I can do that will help me to achieve this?'

INDIVIDUAL ACTIVITY

Knowing myself   Being confident

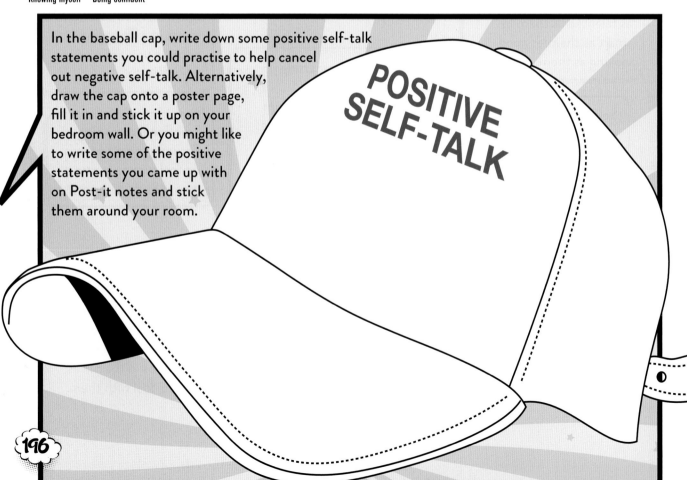

In the baseball cap, write down some positive self-talk statements you could practise to help cancel out negative self-talk. Alternatively, draw the cap onto a poster page, fill it in and stick it up on your bedroom wall. Or you might like to write some of the positive statements you came up with on Post-it notes and stick them around your room.

POSITIVE SELF-TALK

Learning Keepsake

Three things I have learned in this lesson are:

1. _____

2. _____

3. _____

Something that helped me learn in this lesson was:

_____

_____

_____

I could learn even better if:

_____

_____

_____

_____ has shared this Learning Keepsake with me _____

Name of student   *Parent's/Guardian's signature*

Unique and Different Me

LESSON 33

Learning outcomes: 1.1, 1.2

responsible connected respected aware

By the end of this lesson you will:

➤ recognise your own talents and those of others
➤ recognise the importance of contributing to and being mindful of people's self-esteem

KEYWORDS

Assertive

Self-esteem

Confidence

What is self-esteem?

Self-esteem means valuing and respecting yourself as a person. It means recognising your strengths, having respect for yourself and being able to stand up for yourself in an assertive way.

To have healthy self-esteem, it is essential to recognise what you are good at. This is different from being boastful – it means that you know your own strengths. This gives you confidence, and so builds your self-esteem.

INDIVIDUAL ACTIVITY

Knowing myself

Using the letters of your first name, make and decorate a list of the positive things about yourself on a large sheet of paper. Here is Tim's example.

T houghtful towards others
I maginative
M arvellous at rugby!

Co-operating   Listening and expressing myself

PAIR ACTIVITY

In pairs, use the letters of your partner's name to make a list of positive things about them (to do with their personality or talents rather than how they look). Then answer these questions:

1. Was it easy or difficult to come up with your own strengths in the previous task? Give reasons for your answer.

   _____

   _____

2. Was it easy or difficult to come up with your partner's strengths in this task? Why do you think this is?

   _____

   _____

3. What people or things help us to recognise our own strengths?

   _____

   _____

Discussing/ Debating

GROUP ACTIVITY

As a group, discuss and then write down the things that can improve self-esteem and the things that can damage self-esteem.

SELF-ESTEEM BASHERS	SELF-ESTEEM BOOSTERS
Things that make people feel bad about themselves	Things that make people feel good about themselves

Knowing myself

Being confident

INDIVIDUAL ACTIVITY

In the jigsaw below, fill or draw 'the pieces of you' – the different things that make you who you are. When you have finished, compare your jigsaw with those of your classmates. (But only share it if you are comfortable sharing it.)

I am good at

My favourite things

My most memorable experience

My family

My beliefs

My hobbies

I think I am

Sometimes I need help with

My culture

Places I have lived

An accomplishment I am proud of

A person I look up to

My positive self-talk

LEARNING KEEPSAKE

Three things I have learned in this lesson are:

1. _____
2. _____
3. _____

Something that helped me learn in this lesson was:

_____

_____

_____

I could learn even better if:

_____

_____

_____

_____ has shared this Learning Keepsake with me _____

Name of student   *Parent's/Guardian's signature*

MEET THE CHALLENGE

Strand 4 Topic 2
QUIZ – HOW DO I VIEW THE WORLD?

Learning outcomes: 4.8, 4.9

In groups of three, design a quiz for First Years relating to how they view their world. The quiz will establish if they are A. Optimists (try to see the good side of everything); B. Realists (always look at the facts); or C. Pessimists (think the worst will always happen). Your quiz should contain the following elements:

○ at least ten questions relating to different types of situations you might find yourself in

○ three answers for each question, one that the optimist might choose, one that the realist might choose and one that the pessimist might choose

○ instructions for the quiz-taker to count how many As, Bs or Cs they answered

○ a character description for each character type, e.g. 'If you scored mostly As, then you're an optimist. This means that you …'

○ some helpful tips for anyone scoring mostly Cs

TOPIC 3
Loss and Bereavement

Coping with Loss

Learning outcomes: 4.10, 4.11, 4.13

 responsible connected resilient respected aware

By the end of this lesson you will:

•▸ know the different types of loss that happen in people's lives

•▸ understand how to help yourself and others cope with loss

KEYWORDS

Grief

Bereavement

USEFUL WEBSITES

www.barnardos.ie Go to the 'Resources and advice' section for information and support on dealing with loss and bereavement.

www.rainbowsireland.com Offers support programmes for young people who have experienced bereavement, separation or divorce.

www.hospicefoundation.ie Offers information and support for people experiencing bereavement.

CLASS ACTIVITY

Listening/
Expressing
myself

As a class, brainstorm the different losses people might experience.

Dealing with loss

Change is a natural part of life, and change can bring loss. However, with the support of friends and family, a person can cope with the challenges that come with loss.

Although all loss can be difficult to cope with, two of the major losses that might be experienced by a young person are bereavement and parental separation.

Bereavement

Bereavement is a natural part of life but it can be very difficult for young people (or indeed anyone) to cope with. It can cause major upheaval and it takes time to work through the painful feelings of loss and sadness. Grief is the word used to describe our responses and feelings to loss and change in our lives. When we lose someone or something that is important to us, we grieve. Grief is different for everyone and doesn't happen in a set way. The feelings associated with grief can come and go in waves. Many people find they feel a mixture of the following.

anger

relief if the death
followed a long illness

sadness

shock if the death
was unexpected

despair

denial

anxiety

regret

depression

guilt

acceptance

Separation and divorce

Families sometimes break up. Parents who are married may get divorced, co-habiting parents may decide not to live with each other any more. Young people in these families may feel a great deal of hurt and loss if their families break up.

Thinking creatively and critically

Reading with understanding

PAIR ACTIVITY

In pairs, read through Harry's timeline and answer the questions that follow.

Harry is born.

Harry makes friends with Charlie. Harry is very pleased as Charlie is nice. (They are still friends today.)

Harry's dad dies. Harry is heart-broken.

Mum meets Pat. Pat is good fun.

Harry breaks his leg. He is hurt and disappointed because he can't play in the school final.

Harry starts primary school. He is frightened and lonely.

Harry's sister is born and he is excited and jealous.

Harry moves house and he is sad and excited.

Mum marries Pat. Harry is happy.

Harry goes to secondary school and is feeling very nervous.

1. Which change/loss do you think Harry found the most difficult? Give reasons for your answer.

_____

_____

_____

2. Who or what could have helped Harry to cope with the changes and losses in his life?

_____

_____

_____

3. What advice would you give to Harry as he starts secondary school?

_____

_____

_____

Tips for coping with serious loss or bereavement

It is important to know that there is help available and that a young person can use some self-help strategies to cope with difficult times.

- ☞ If you have a trusted adult in your life, you can speak to them and ask them for support and advice.

- ☞ You can attend a group like Rainbows. Most schools have a Rainbows group and you can enquire in your school about it.

- ☞ Look after your physical health, try to sleep well, eat well and exercise.

- ☞ Seeing your friends and keeping in touch with your social groups is important.

- ☞ Be patient with yourself. Everyone experiences grief differently, and everyone's journey through grief will be different.

- ☞ Find coping strategies that best suit you.

- ☞ Keep a journal to record your feelings as this can have a very therapeutic effect.

- ☞ In the case of bereavement, do special things to help keep the memory of a loved one alive, for example, plant a tree, write a letter, or do something in their honour like compete in a race.

Knowing myself

Being confident/ spiritual

INDIVIDUAL ACTIVITY

Now fill in your own timeline. In the numbered boxes, write any change or loss that has occurred in your life and what age you were. Only include things that you feel comfortable talking about. In the white boxes above or below the numbered boxes, write in what helped you cope in each situation.

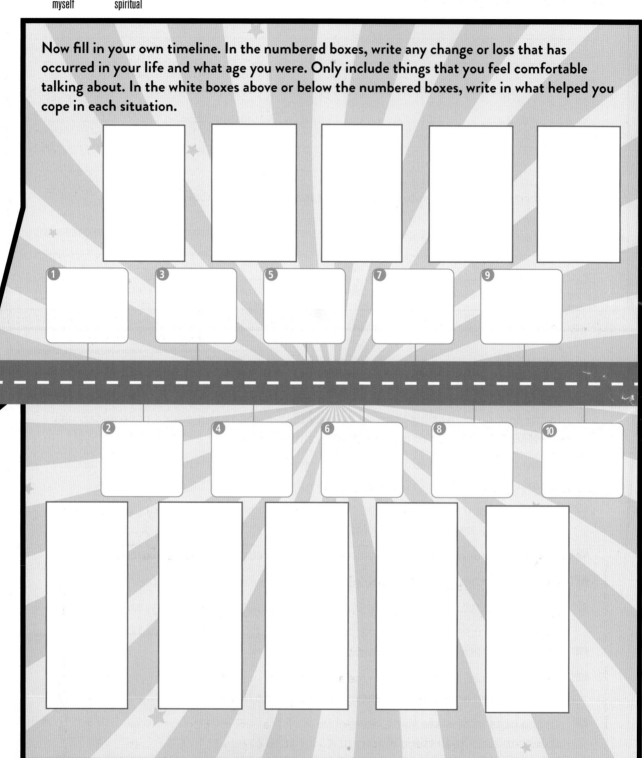

How to help someone experiencing change or loss

Sometimes it can be difficult to know what to say or do if someone you know has experienced a loss. The following may be helpful.

Do	Don't
Tell them you are there for them if they want to talk or meet up.	Avoid them because you are worried they might be upset. Think about how grateful you would be if they were there for you.
Be prepared to see them go through different emotions; it is usual for bereaved people or people experiencing other types of loss or change to feel guilt and anger as part of the grieving process.	Force them to talk to you if they don't want to. Suggest they talk to a counsellor or a trusted adult if you feel they need to talk to someone.
Try to offer practical help, e.g. with notes or homework, etc.	Stop inviting them to things, even if they don't want to take part.
Allow them to cry if they feel they want to.	Pass judgement if they are full of self-pity; this is a part of the grieving process.
Encourage them to give themselves plenty of time: grief has no set timeline.	Tell them that they should be feeling better by now.
If the person is bereaved, talk about the good qualities that their loved one had.	Try to find something positive about the loss, e.g. that it could have been worse.
Take care of them during special occasions like Christmas, anniversaries, etc. as these times can make their grief worse.	Say you know how they feel if you don't.

Where to go for help and support

- Your school counsellor or chaplain will be able to talk to you if you are experiencing bereavement, loss, separation or divorce in your life and need to speak with someone in a trusting and confidential environment.

- **www.childline.ie** A 24-hour helpline and online service offering information and support for young people and teenagers. **Freephone 1800 666 666**.

- **www.rainbowsireland.ie** The Rainbows network is a peer support group for people of all ages who have experienced death, separation or divorce in their lives.

- **www.barnardos.ie** Barnardos' bereavement helpline operates from 10 a.m.–12 p.m. Monday to Friday. Tel: 01 473 2110.

- **www.teenline.ie** TeenLine Ireland is a non-profit helpline aimed at young people aged 13–19. Freephone 1800 833 634 or free text TEEN to 50015.

- **www.childhoodbereavement.ie** Irish Childhood Bereavement Network provides guidance and support for young people to help them to manage the impact of death in their lives. Tel: 01 679 3188 or message them on their website.

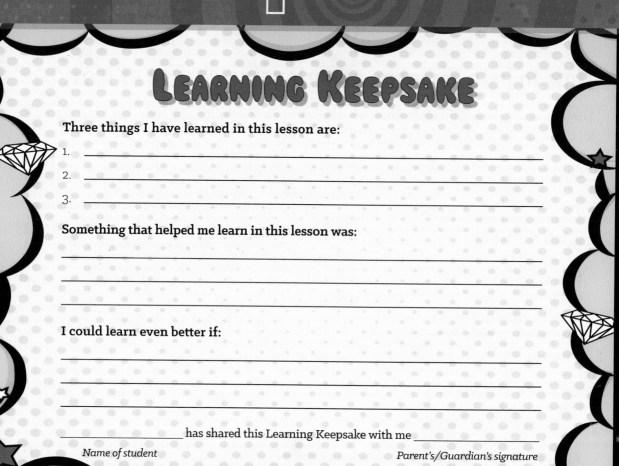

LEARNING KEEPSAKE

Three things I have learned in this lesson are:

1. _____

2. _____

3. _____

Something that helped me learn in this lesson was:

_____

_____

_____

I could learn even better if:

_____

_____

_____

_____ has shared this Learning Keepsake with me _____

Name of student   *Parent's/Guardian's signature*

MEET THE CHALLENGE
Strand 4 Topic 3
WRITE A POEM ON CHANGE OR LOSS

Learning outcomes: 4.8, 4.9, 4.11, 4.13

Write a poem or a personal essay about how you managed an important change/ loss in your life. In your writing, talk about:

○ how you felt during this time

○ someone or something that helped you deal with the change/loss you experienced

○ advice you would give to someone if they were going through something similar